CW00552502

The
Southern Way

The regular volume for the Southern devotee

Kevin Robertson

Issue 41

31924

www.crecy.co.uk

© 2018 Crécy Publishing Ltd
and the various contributors

ISBN 9781909328747

First published in 2018 by Noodle Books
an imprint of Crécy Publishing Ltd

All editorial submissions to:
The Southern Way (Kevin Robertson)
Conway
Warnford Rd
Corhampton
Hants SO32 3ND
Tel: 01489 877880
editorial@thesouthernway.co.uk

Publisher's note: Every effort has been made to
identify and correctly attribute photographic
credits. Any error that may have occurred is
entirely unintentional.
In line with the new design the front cover image has
changed from that originally advertised. All other
information is unaffected.

Printed in England by LatimerTrend

Noodle Books is an imprint of
Crécy Publishing Limited
1a Ringway Trading Estate
Shadowmoss Road
Manchester M22 5LH

www.crecy.co.uk

Issue No 42 of THE SOUTHERN WAY
ISBN 9781909328761
available in April 2018 at £14.95

To receive your copy the moment it is
released, order in advance from your usual
supplier, or it can be sent post-free (UK)
direct from the publisher:

Crécy Publishing Ltd

1a Ringway Trading Estate, Shadowmoss
Road, Manchester M22 5LH

Tel 0161 499 0024

www.crecy.co.uk

enquiries@crecy.co.uk

Front Cover:
Not surprisingly, this particular view seemed appropriate
for this, the first issue of 2018. 'Standard 5', or to quote
Peter Smith in *Mendips Enginemen*, one of the 'Fabulous
Fives', No 73049 arriving at Blandford southbound with
what is clearly a local working. Whilst no doubt
appreciative of the ease an engine of this type would have
likely worked such a short train, the economics of such a
move must be questioned, unless of course it was a filling
in turn for the loco between more arduous duties. There
is no date for when it was taken but No 73049 was
allocated to Bath Green Park Between August 1955 and
April 1960 and then again from July 1962 until either
September or October 1964, after which it went to Oxford
and was withdrawn in March 1965. The view is one of
several originally from the collection of the late Tony
Woodforth – ex Basingstoke driver, and sadly missed.

Rear cover:
The one that didn't make it. LNER 'V2' No 60919 at
Basingstoke shed on 29 June 1966. The engine had
travelled south all the way from Dundee ready to take
the LCGB 'Green Arrow' tour of 3 July 1966 but instead
was failed and local candidate No 34002 was
substituted. (The 'V2' was still on the books of the
Eastern/Scottish Region until withdrawn a few weeks
later on 2 September 1966.) *B H Jackson*

Title page:
We have been privileged over the years to receive
occasional batches of photographs from various
individuals (I nearly wrote 'odd' there, but that would
certainly not have been intended as it might have first
read). One of these worthies is David Linsell, who in a
recent batch submitted the attached view of a 'W', No
31924, running light and heading west under Battledown
Flyover. Although undated it is reasonable to assume this
was around late November 1962 when the engine was
transferred from Feltham to Exmouth Junction and used
for banking duties there. It would return to the London
area a year later, this time to Norwood Junction.
Jeffrey Saunders/David Linsell collection

Contents

Introduction

Readers will no doubt be aware that I spent the last five years of my life working for Ian Allan Publishing, a role that I was privileged to have been offered and equally privileged to undertake. Most will also be aware that IA closed its publishing operation at the end of 2016 and, like those of us who remained until the end, I was made redundant at that time. Redundancy is a sad fact of life in modern society. I bear no grudge against my former employer, these things happen, as fashions, markets and businesses change. Indeed, I am well aware of countless railwaymen who roles were lost and who either accepted redundancy and so lost the railway as an employer or were forced to reapply for roles and positions sometimes outside their established own comfort zone. Let me say also that there were those who then developed and shone, rising far above where their old position might have led. I think it was also Adrian Vaughan who once said, 'There are not many vacancies for railway firemen or railway signalmen at the Labour Exchange these days.' I will also admit this was not the first time it had happened to me in my working career, the third time in fact, but life goes on and the old saying of, 'one door closes …' and all that.

So, to repeat my oft-quoted phrase, 'Where is this leading?' – well I will tell you, and that is a discussion about where our railway hobby, and especially our book hobby, is going.

Back in 1968 I am told that Ian Allan (and likely others) had some concern that the consequential end of steam would also coincide with the end of the railway book market. As we all know, that did not happen; indeed the plethora of books and publishers that have graced and sometimes fallen by the wayside since are testimony to the continuing interest that has developed post-steam on BR. Indeed, I think it fair to say that my own library shelves contain far more that has been published since that time than before. Likewise the model market. Back in 1968 it was Tri-ang who dominated the ready-to-run market, having then recently swallowed up Hornby-Dublo, with kit, scratch building, and the likes of 'O' gauge and others accounting for only a very small percentage of interest.

But fifty years later and the position is very different. There are, or have been, models for certainly all the major classes and many of the lesser engine types as well. Similarly rolling stock. Certainly those of us without the skills to build to the standards of the late Guy Williams (and his equivalent in coach/wagon building) are spoilt for choice. Books too have come and gone, but most branch lines and a fair proportion of main lines have been covered at least once, locomotive types also, leaving

The fiftieth LMS 2-8-0 built at Brighton for the LMS. No 8645 photographed in 1943.

perhaps only a few topics where there still remain gaps for original research. Indeed, I recall a few years being responsible for the rejection of a colossal manuscript, as I recall something in the order of 400,000 words, on the history and development of the steam engine as just something that was simply not commercially viable. I do have a conscience and I genuinely felt awful as I signed the letter saying, 'Thank you – but No thank you', especially as the contributor had stated it represented his life's work – and I could well believe him as well. (For comparison sake, the average detailed branch line book of, say, 160 sides might have 80,000 words.) So, is there a future for railway books and models? So far as the model side is concerned I am not involved in that market but there are clearly those who believe there is and I sincerely wish them good luck. As a commercial proposition it matters not who you sell your product to, his/her age, gender, religion – all the other criteria into which we are now seemingly neatly compartmentalised – what matters is that it sells. So good luck to Hornby, Bachmann, Dapol and the smaller manufacturers who are prepared to have a go; your confidence and your courage is an inspiration to us all.

And so I turn to the book market. With the fifty-year anniversary end of Southern steam recalled in 2017 and the same for BR steam as a whole to come this year, is there a place for more of the printed word in years to come, or are we either sated or about to be? If one looks at the number of 'new' tiles being

produced the answer has to be there are publishers out there who believe there is still a market, and I am also one who sincerely hopes there is. I say this not, I assure you, from any selfish perspective but instead because many of the older books, once considered the standard works on their respective subject, are either unknown to the current market or simply unobtainable. Similarly, what was acceptable fifty years ago, basically text with a few separate sections of illustrations, is not tolerated today.

I would hope though that a reworking of an old subject will also add to the pool of knowledge and not simply be a rehash of the old, sometimes including comments that have since been proven to be wrong. By all means push the boundaries but there should still be a clearly defined difference between quoted and proven fact and supposition or opinion. The latter two are certainly welcome, but back them up with reasoned argument. That way the new will better likely stand the test of time. I should say also the same applies with articles in this and other periodicals; they should mention when and where information has come from and why an argument today is different from yesterday. To me and I know others, this is where the likes of various search engines have their weakness. Most are indeed accurate but because it appears on Google it 'must be right'. It becomes ever more difficult then to correct an error from the past that is proven to be wrong simply because such inaccuracies have managed to cross the boundary into fact.

Through the good offices of long-time *SW* friend, Colin Martin, we can present another image with a definite connection to *SW*. Roads named after various locomotive designers are relatively common, although it is sad to think that perhaps not all the residents thereof would have a clue as to who Messrs. Walker, Cubitt, or Maunsell were. Personally I also cringe every time I see a new development known as 'The Sidings' or such like; to me a cheap means of paying lip service to what was formerly a railway area. But just east of the station at Farnham – well what can I say … I will though have to admit this particular residential road was in existence some years before this journal. We started *SW* the periodical in 2007, the road appears to date back to 1995. I can only say there was no deliberate plagiarism. The name *SW* came up as an idea a year or so before the first issue and, as for Noodle Books, well at the time we kept chickens and one of them was named Noodle. I think at this point I had better stop (before getting ever more scrambled than ever).

To some it also seems fashionable to knock the writers of the past purely because they were from an earlier generation. I will name two from yesteryear, Messrs Nock and Allan, and purely because they are probably the best-known names of their time. So ask the question: were the histories produced by these men inaccurate, were they wrong to often concentrate on the performance of the engines rather than looking at the broader picture? I say no, what they did was provide a grounding on which others have subsequently built far stronger foundations. But just as it was important yesterday, so caution should be exercised today in jumping to conclusions without considering all the facts. I will give one example, a personal one if I may. On a recent discussion group there was some debate over my own pet subject, No 36001 and her sisters. Now put aside the odd word I have written on this topic in the past, I am not a mechanical engineer, I do not profess to be and I also readily accept there are those who likely know the subject at least as well as I do. But what was stated recently made me sit up somewhat. This was a suggestion that the steel and other metals used in the construction of 'Leader' were sub-standard and this was the reason it failed. Said contributor completed his view by stating that sub-standard steel was rife after the Second World War. It is an interesting hypothesis and it did rekindle discussion. Regrettably, no one responded with what to me was the obvious. Had this been the case then surely the batch of Pacifics being built at Brighton at the same time would likely have suffered similar problems. They did not. So we have it, an interesting idea that now rests in the minds of some but to me at least does not appear to have been thought through. Am I being defensive on the subject, well some would say yes, but if it appears that way it is not intended. I would love to know more about 'the beast', but new information must be backed up. In the same way, I genuinely do welcome discussion, we can never know it all. What was recorded in the minute books and records can only be the conclusions of discussions and debate. But for debate and view to come out on top there must be the opportunity to present the opposite perspective. This is hopefully where *SW* and Rebuilt have their place, as an open forum to all. And please, if you wish to come back to me then do so.

So to conclude, and besides this particular soap box is getting decidedly wobbly, You will note I have deliberately not referred to the merits or otherwise of railway history being produced in hard copy verses electronic form. How you decide to satisfy your appetite is entirely your opinion. We live in an age where it is wonderful to have the wealth of information that is currently available at our fingertips, but as I have oft quoted in the past, there is still a vast archive not online nor probably ever likely to be (certainly in my lifetime). It is this great treasure trove that could yet reveal many secrets. (Perhaps next time I should also go for a shorter intro piece, they seem to be getting longer with each issue!)

Engineering the Southern
Waterloo May 1942 to July 1944 and Brighton July 1944 to 1950, Harold Attwell
Compiled by Jeremy Staines

H. W. Butler in his office at Brighton. Do we dare comment about the GWR 4-6-0 having pride of place in the centre of the three photographs on the wall behind …? Mr Butler had never worked for the GWR! *Howard Butler*

There were thousands of men who made up the Southern Railway. At the top the names of Bulleid, Walker, Elliott, Missenden, Maunsell and others will immediately be familiar, whilst further down artisans engaged in the actual physical operation of the railway are unlikely to be well known, except perhaps by their peers or immediate colleagues.

In all layers in between came the men (and women) who were responsible for the implementation of the policies and dictates of their masters. Some of these are names we are again familiar with: Sykes, Holcroft, Townroe, Granshaw, etc,

names that have often been referred to in the pages of *SW* and elsewhere. Again their longevity may well be sometimes attributed to a few words previously recorded and perhaps unearthed in more recent times, or even due to the actions of a modern day sleuth.

Other names, though, remain a mystery. Books from decades past mention a name, perhaps a position or even a veiled hint at the actions, of 'A N Other', tantalisingly without further reference to the individual concerned.

It is with one of these men that this article is concerned; Harold Ware Attwell, who held a senior position within the Testing Section at Brighton in the late 1940s and so was immediately involved in the fascinating innovations taking place at the time.

Let me say straight away what follows is actual original text, and not something that I have put together from pieces of information. It was written longhand, almost as if part of a letter or notes, perhaps intended to assist another or even to form the basis for an article or book at some stage in the future. The material did not come from the family or any known descendent, instead it was located purely by chance in an archive totally unrelated to the name. Whether this is all that exists, or there happens to be more elsewhere, we cannot be certain. What we can be sure of is that without an apparent introduction we have to accept that it just 'wades in' and stops in similar fashion. However, it certainly leaves me, and I hope the reader, wanting more, that is if there is more to be found – there certainly is not in the same source where this was located.

There were no illustrations,[1] just twenty-four pages of handwritten notes, some alluding also to further text, but as we say this has not been found. Even so, the material is literally dynamite to the modern day researcher. Questions are answered (and, of course, others raised) often contradicting (should that not now be correcting?) previously stated fact.

The text is shown below almost exactly as written, the only changes made being for grammatical purposes or to clarify a point. In most cases where this has taken place today's comments are shown in parenthesis. I am sure the readers of *SW* will be as equally enthralled by what follows as I was reading it for the first time many miles away from Southern territory:

'Under the leadership of C.S. Cocks the transferred staff from Eastleigh and Brighton commenced work on the technical aspects of building the LMS 8F 2-8-0 at the SR Works. This included our proposals for fabricating by welding some of the details, all of which were eventually turned down by Derby.' (*The writer's own comment in brackets now follows:* 'a piece of SR impertinence?') There was also the inauguration of progress meetings to co-ordinate production at Ashford, Brighton and Eastleigh works and issue of an SDR (?) building schedule to tie up with the LMS building schedule to assist for costing purposes. Materials ordering was also a priority and an excellent liaison was built up with the Stores Dept, who made prodigious efforts to meet our requirements with very short delivery dates.

Cocks named me as his deputy and I was involved in all aspects of the foregoing, although efforts to obtain assistance from other works such as Derby and Stratford met with no success.

By this time the USA had begun involvement in the European war and had requested the appointment of a railway representative to co-ordinate the arrival of their railroad equipment. A former C&W Dept colleague, S.G. Smith at the Ministry of Supply, had recommended me and U.S. Colonel Bingham arrived at Waterloo to arrange my secondment to the U.S. Transportation Corps. OVB would not agree and another member of our staff (H. L. Butler) took up the post. The Waterloo office however, was called in from time to time in connection with mirror modifications to the American 2-8-0s. (*See also SW Issue No 2, with information on H. L. Butler.*)

As work on the foregoing projects tailed off OVB began investigating the requirement for building the second ten 'Merchant Navy' engines, to be numbered 21C11–21C20. One project was for the use of fabricated wheels in place of the B.F.B. steel castings which had been found overweight but in the event although I made drawings only one set was manufactured for trial. Drawings were also made for the LMS 2-8-0 coupled wheels but this did not get beyond the design stage. (*Here the text is not completely clear, does the writer mean that BFB wheels were considered for the 2-8-0s?*)

OVB had been concerned about smoke lifting on the first ten M.N. class and a number of films were made by the S.R. Publicity Dept film unit showing these locos in service. The cab windows were seen to be obscured by smoke to a large extent and when the second ten were built the front end casing was modified to include a short outer down draught shield having some resemblance to those fitted on other S.R. locos. I maintained that a longer plate would be more effective but Cocks derided this and although the short plates mitigated the smoke nuisance to some extent, I was eventually able to get longer plates fitted which were indeed much more effective.

The inside cylinder was modified to incorporate a cast balance pipe and as difficulties had been experienced with fractures of smokebox steam and exhaust pipes the former were modified with corrugations and the latter with bellows. Teething troubles occurred with these modified pipes but were eventually overcome. The cab and tender layouts were also improved for greater obvious comfort, that of the tender mainly to give better read observation. The front ring of the boiler band was made parallel instead of being tapered at bottom toward the front tubeplate.

The infant Waterloo design office was not popular at Eastleigh, in particular partly owing to the drive of C.S. Cocks, whose tough methods were not always appreciated. They sometimes shook individuals not particularly welcoming change, an example of this being the building schedule for the second ten M.N, type which for the first time included every item down to the smallest nut, bolt and screw with an appropriate sub-number for manufacturing or costing purpose.

A poor rendition but nevertheless likely unique view of part of the Brighton drawing office. *Howard Butler*

The first 'Leader' under construction. Much could be said about this image but which would likely repeat what has been said elsewhere. Suffice it to say boiler, mantle tank and bunker are in position, the former two items offset from the frame centre line by 9in. To the right is the circular frame used to assist in welding the bogie components. Two casings that will later form part of the outside of the bogies live upturned on the workshop floor. I am sure the editor will not mind a plug for his later but now out of print book, *The Leader Project: Fiasco or Triumph? (Thank you not at all – Ed!)*

For example, a blast pipe cap, which would come in section 6B (Section 6 covering smokeboxes), the cap and details being items 6B14–24 inclusive. This splitting of detail was the cause of an irate senior member of the Eastleigh costing office storming into Waterloo and stating categorically that most of the men in the works would be incapable of understanding such hair splitting and that the result would be confusion and inaccuracies. Nothing further was heard and the methods used continued until the Derby takeover of the design function in 1967.

During 1943 consideration was given to a locomotive, second only in power to the M.N., for working over the parts of the SR system where weight or other restrictions prevented the M.N. from working. An early version was a 4-6-0 of similar capacity to an LMS class 5MT 4-6-0 but this was quickly abandoned in favour of a 'lightweight' 4-6-2 later christened the 'West Country' class. The total diagram weight was 86 tons, total wheelbase 57' 6", capable of being turned on 60' turntables, max width 8' 6" to suit working on the Tonbridge–Hastings line and route availability over 88% of the S.R. system. (*The writer adds again in brackets:* The Q1 was capable of working over 93% of the S.R. but was restricted to a max. speed of 55 mph. I have timed them at 70! Their brake power was only equivalent to the less powerful Q class as previously explained and would have been unsatisfactory for heavy freight workings).

While many of the details were identical with the M.N., it was necessary to design frame stretchers, hauling truck, etc, as welded structures in order to be within the 86 tonnes and every detail was checked to keep weight down. When the first loco was completed and weighed at Brighton coincidentally on the day of the European war ending in May 1945 the estimated weight was achieved.

The first sign of development toward the 'Leader' emerged in 1943/4 when some preliminary design work was carried out by our F. J. R. Watts on high-speed engines. These were essentially for use on power bogies which would be replaceable units. No decision was reached on the use of these units.

During June 1944 the 'flying bomb' attacks caused many hold-ups in the work of the Department and it was decided that the office should be moved to the old LBSCR offices at Brighton, where work continued with little interruption. OVB remained at Waterloo and I returned there during December 1944 and January 1945 to assist where necessary.

During 1946 the fuel situation had become difficult and to replace coal a national railway project was instigated to fit a number of locos as oil burners. The basic details for locos were worked out at Swindon and applied at Brighton to suit SR requirements but by the time the fitting was in full swing the coal position had eased and the work on SR was restricted to 31 locos as at 26 September 1947. One 'West Country' was fitted with the standard arrangement but due to the short firebox the results were unsatisfactory. Experiments were continued to improve the arrangement and these appeared to be within success when cancelled by BR following nationalisation. I was not involved in the loco side but dealt with installations at depots.

Cocks had persuaded OVB that the duties of a double bogie loco he was considering could more easily be performed by locos of more conventional wheel arrangements such as a 4-6-4 tank and others. However, the idea of a watertube firebox was examined and I spent some time developing a welded boiler of this type. Welding problems proved difficult to overcome, mainly due to access, and this scheme was dropped.

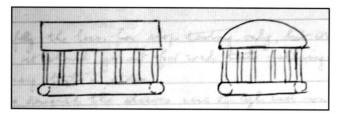

Within the written text were a few hand drawings, including this one of what the water tube boiler arrangement may have been like. (Reminiscent of a Roman coliseum even!). In all seriousness though, Bulleid would have been aware from his own time on the LNER of the work and performance of the LNER 'W1' 4-6-4 fitted with this type of boiler. Could this be why he considered the idea for the Southern? Yet again, it is an example of how little we know of Bulleid work on the LNER.

OVB had become interested in the possibility of using sleeve-valve cylinders based on the 'Bristol' aircraft engine and he obtained copies of the journal 'Aircraft Production' which gave details of the valves. The journals were passed to me with instructions to develop a valve suitable for steam locos. When the first scheme was produced, Ricardo was called in for comment and he approved the general layout with the exception that the normal reciprocatory movement should be modified to have a semi-rotary movement to avoid scoring of surfaces.

The next development was to fit a loco and a 'King Arthur' 4-6-0 was suggested but incorporating a sleeve valve increased the width over the cylinders to an extent sufficient to foul the load gauge. (*The Editor recalls being told by S. C. Townroe that the SR Motive Power department fought and won so as not to give up a 'King Arthur', the type being considered as useful and reliable. The alternative suggestion being that OVB should use one of his own engines …!*)

Looking round for an alternative produced an 'H1' class 'Atlantic' which was due for scrap and No 2039 of this class was selected for modification. (*By this do we then imply that the 'King Arthur' had also been due for scrap?*) The original intention was to modify the loco for shop testing only, but OVB decided that it should go out for road tests following satisfactory stationary tests in steam. As designed the sleeves were of cylinder cast iron (and heavy) with projecting 'ears' through the front cylinder covers to take the drives.

Temperature and dimensional checks were made to ascertain any deformation of the sleeves, the temperatures usually being in the range 200–250°. At an early stage breakage of the 'ears' of the sleeves occurred and as a 'fail safe' measure the main steel drive pins were replaced by hollow bronze pins with walls 1/10' thick. During following tests in Brighton Erecting shop with the loco on rollers, I observed the behaviour of the sleeves and on only one occasion did it appear there was likelihood of seizure. The bronze pin was slightly dented. (*Presumably the use of the hollow bronze allowed a degree of flexibility compared with the steel.*) When the loco went on the road with the bronze pins in position there were no breakage difficulties although lubrication was not always satisfactory.

I have one record of sleeve and liner dimensions taken after breakage as follows:

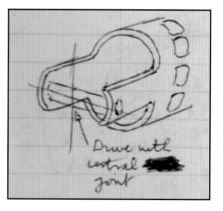

The second of the drawings this showing the end of a sleeve and indicating where the bronze pin was inserted through the 'ears'. (Just one of the set of steam openings in the sleeve are shown as a series of cuts around the main circumference.)

LC Cyl	A1 = 15.745	B1 = 15.7435	A1 = 15.751	B1 = 15.751
	A2 = 15.746	B2 = 15.743	A2 = 15.754	B2 = 15.749
	A3 = 15.744	B3 = 15.743	A3 = 15.751	B3 = 15.748
	A4 = 15.744	B4 = 15.742	A4 = 15.7495	B4 =15.751
RH Cyl	A1 = 15.744	B1 = 15.742	A1 = 15.749	B1 = 15.7505
	A2 = 15.7435	B2 = 15.743	A2 = 15.749	B2 = 15.749
	A3 = 15.740	B3 = 15.740	A3 = 15.751	B3 = 15.750
	A4 = 15.741	B4 = 15.742	A4 = 15.7515	B4 = 15.749

There were no rings fitted at this stage.

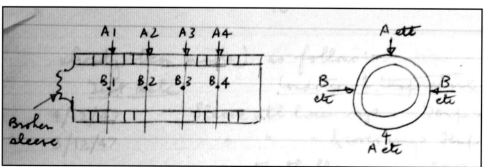

The original writer's sketch of where the sleeve measurements were taken from.

OVB decided that the loco should be taken out and run on a works siding without rings and invited H.G. Ivatt to observe. This occurred on 3 December 1947 and the loco was enveloped in clouds of steam. HGI was amused but OVB was not. The maximum temperature was taken as 235°C. There were no more tests without rings but a programme was inaugurated with rings (for which provision had already been made) as follows:

Test Date	Condition & Temperature etc
4/12/47	Sleeve with liner rings. Temp 250°C.
8/12/47	Sleeve with liner rings and cover rings. Temp 275°C.
10/12/47	Sleeve etc with all rings. No temperature record.
13/12/47	20 trips on siding as 10/12. Temp 235°C. Steam leakage practically eliminated. Bronze drive pins on above and all subsequent tests.
15/12/47	To Lewes and return. Without chain drive from Falmer and hauled by another loco. Minor trouble not recalled.
20/12/47	To Lewes and return with other loco as precaution. No trouble.
22 & 23/12/47	To Eastbourne then Pevensey and return. OK. Lub set a min feed.
29/12/47	To Eastbourne then Pevensey and return. Lub at max feed – not satisfactory.
30/12/47	To Haywards Heath and return. Lub unsatisfactory.
31/12/47	To Haywards Heath and return. Lub satisfactory.
1/1/48	To Three Bridges and return via Hove. Lub satisfactory.

I have no further records but I made one journey with a 3-coach train to Eastbourne and return. We had a young fireman who was 'green' and could not get much steam but the loco behaved well although losing time. Agreed it was due for scrap but could have done better. However, OVB went with this light train to Ashford and it was reported that 80 mph was attained! After this the loco was considered to have fulfilled its purpose and was scrapped. *(Not strictly true, as 2039 was later employed on a regular empty stock working from Lancing to Eastleigh. Even so the writer has for the very first time provided us with detail of some of the road trials undertaken by No 2039 – fascinating!)*

While the sleeve valve was being developed, the schemes for the tank locos had multiplied without any decision being made, but one fateful day in the absence of Cocks, I was called to OVB's office and requested to produce a sketch for a double wheeled bogie loco. This scheme as with many others before and after was made by J.G. Jones. On his return Cocks was not pleased, but once the decision was made, pressed on with development. Early layouts showed bogie frames inside the wheels but I found that it was impossible to get 3-cylinders in line – these would have been piston valve cylinders with the centre cylinder inclined and the outer cylinders horizontal – so the frames were altered to box section outside the wheels. The bogies were also not long enough to get sleeve valve cylinders clear of the outer axles as the frames had to be lengthened. The overall length of the locomotive shown in what OVB once stated in a paper was the preliminary designs – drg W7457, although this was not the first scheme, was increased from 59' to 67' over buffers.

Top right: **No 2039 in the process of being fitted out at Brighton on 17 March 1947. Assuming the date of the photographer to have been recorded correctly, then this means it was almost another nine months before the engine actually emerged in steam in front of Ivatt and Bulleid. Did it really take all this time to complete the work or were shop trials actually carried out in the meanwhile? Yet again it proves the point that whilst new information is indeed welcome it sometimes, as here, throws up questions that had been considered before.**

Top left: **No 2039 in steam at Eastleigh having brought its weekly train of carriage underframes from Lancing. This was its regular duty and it must be said there is no record of it having failed on the duty, although it was reported water stops had to be made literally at every location where a water column was provided. Despite it being on the supposed condemned list, in 1947 the engine was subsequently overhauled and given a replacement boiler by BR, at the same time being repainted and acquiring the number No 32039. In this form it did even less work and was indeed laid aside and scrapped soon afterwards.**

Right: **No 2039 complete and recorded at Brighton on 17 March 1949. What we do not know is how many trips were being made with the engine at this time or if all effort was being concentrated on her sister, No 36001. Whatever, the complexities of the oscillating sleeve valve operations are clearly visible.**

OVB foreshadowed the production of these locos in his Presidential address to the I.MechE on 18 October 1946 when he gave the considerations required in the design.

Originally the cylinders were 13¼" diameter x 15" stroke giving a tractive force of 30,800lb but due to the limited space available to accommodate sleeve valve cylinders the diameter was reduced to 12¼' with a tractive force of 26,300lb. One feature of the sleeve valve design was a cylinder clearance volume of little more than 6% compared with approx. 10% with piston valve locos of the period. Time was not on the side of an unconventional design of this nature as it was realised that lighter sleeves would have obviated some of the problems found compared with the cast iron sleeves, but although consideration was given to suitable materials for lighter sleeves nothing was developed in time for production.

I have mentioned in discussion the early scheme for cylinders open-ended between pistons with slidebars and crossheads centralised beneath as per the sketch. *(Regrettably there is no sketch, but we do know that this same type of 'double-acting' piston arrangement was later considered for the 'Turfburner', although again rejected.)*

Drawings were completed but the disadvantages are obvious and they were soon relegated to obscurity.

As the loco has been described elsewhere I will not deal with other features such as the boiler, particularly as John Click has been in communication with other former members of the Brighton office involved in the design.

A quarter size model of the cylinders and motion, sectioned where necessary was manufactured at Lancing works and was eventually handed over to the B.R. Archivist. I do not know now whether it is in their possession – it should be – together with all the drawings of the locomotive.

By the spring of 1949 No 36001 the first of the five locos ordered, the original proposal was for 45, *(Here the writer quotes a figure no else has confirmed. It is likely this should really be 31)* and in production was ready for trial. It was not long before sleeve leakage occurred and arrangements were made for members of the design and testing staffs to travel situated at each end of the loco, with the platform removed over the sleeve valve driving gear, in order to observe behaviour of the valves in operation, one man to each cylinder. Rumours had circulated following production of the first bogie later installed beneath the smokebox, that Brighton works had tested this bogie and that some damage had occurred but the works remained tight-lipped and nothing was proved. *(Again this was reported to your editor years ago. L. J. Granshaw, the Brighton Works Manager, had a completed bogie raised off the ground and supplied with steam from a nearby engine. It ran perfectly. But then he instructed that it be reversed before fully coming to a halt. Damage was caused but this was repaired apparently without OVB ever learning of the episode.)*

No 36001 on trial at Lewes. No 1 end (smoke box) is leading and it will be noted the covers to the oscillating gear have been removed. The curved steps were necessary to gain access to – or exit – the cab should the locomotive be stopped on a curve. Whilst no doubt a considered view on the part of the drawing office, in practice men would invariably complain the design was such as to cause a whack on the shins on many occasions.

I took part in all the early road tests from Brighton to Uckfield or Seaford for instance and later with a train from Brighton via Uckfield on a scheduled through journey to Victoria which was terminated at Oxted due to steam shortage. Our usual fireman was not available and a youngster, the only one available, who had no experience of the loco did not come up to scratch. The 'Leader' had been designed to take water from Western Section columns and had difficulty at Oxted in obtaining a supply from the LBSCR type, this also at stations on the return journey to Brighton via Sheffield Park where we were able to fill up. Incidentally the loco was not officially allowed to run over this return route.

Returning to the valve observations it was noticeable that the valves operating at the smokebox (hot) end did not sound so sweet in comparison with the opposite (cool) end, the comment being that the latter ran like a sewing machine. No difficulties ever occurred at this end.

A trial run from Brighton to Eastleigh with train was arranged later in the summer and apart from a blowing cylinder cock which was attended to at Angmering, causing some delay, no trouble was experience. I was not on the return journey when the loco broke down in the Worthing area.

By this time design work on the BR Standard loco had commenced at Brighton and test work on the 'Leader' was put in charge of L. J. Granshaw, the Brighton Works Manager whose relations with C. S. Cocks had been far from cordial. There had been dissension between them on the course to adopt on various aspects of manufacture and difficulties sometimes in the presence of OVB and I had been called in by the latter when an impasse had been reached. Granshaw had endeavoured much earlier to restrict the Drawing Office from access to Brighton Works and had been overruled by OVB. When OVB left the Southern in autumn 1949 our contact with the 'Leader' was minimal and the last occasion a conference with all concerned took place at Brighton was on 15 December 1949.

At this conference OVB agreed with my contention that we would have done better to stick to conventional cylinders and boiler to prove the project. *(This is followed by some very brief text which makes no sense but it is clear there was no love lost between some of the participants as the sentence concludes with the words),* '… Cocks' remarks that Hutchinson never knows what he is talking about'.[2]

Reverting to design, the offsetting of the boiler from the longitudinal centre line had caused difficulties with weigh distribution and in any case the loco was much heavier than the design figure, which I do not now recollect.

Owing to the offset, the weight on one side was greater than the other and for one weighing the side corridor was partly filled with cast iron blocks to even the distribution, which made the total weight even greater. The fuel capacity was 4,000 gallons of water and 4 tons of coal but at a later stage this was reduced to 3,000 gallons and 3 tons. I made a weighing in this condition but without blocks in corridor at Brighton on 31/1/1950 and I attach a copy of the results. As only 5 tables were available (as on other SR weighbridges) each bogie was weighted independently and moved along the tables to obtain 6 complete weighings (3 per bogie) as shown on the diagrams. Note how the weight at any position varied when moved from table to table. In these conditions the design route availability of 97% or remotely approaching this figure would have been unobtainable and a complete rethink necessary for future locos. My final connection with 36001 came on 20 June 1950 when I visited Eastleigh Works to check valve events.

Weighing	No 1 end (smokebox)	Weigh-tables						No 2 end (tank and bunker)
		1	2	3	4	5		
		11-4-2	11-18-3 3	11-1-1			Total 34-4-2	
1		No 1 bogie. No 2 bogie off tables						61-18-0
			7-13-0	8-15-3	11-4-3		Total 27-13-2	
			11-9-3	11-11-1	10-6-3		Total 33-7-3	
2		No 1 bogie. No 2 bogie off tables						62-16-1
			7-18-0	10-1-3	11-8-3		Total 29-8-2	
			10-15-0	10-16-3	10-17-2		Total 32-9-1	
3			No 1 bogie. No 2 bogie off tables					62-16-1
	No 1 bogie off tables		7-18-0	10-1-3	11-8-3		Total 29-6-1	
			9-2-0	10-3-0	11-17-3		Total 31-2-3	
4			No 2 bogie					66-1-2
	No 1 bogie off tables		12-2-3	11-2-3	11-13-1		Total 34-18-3	
			11-13-2	11-15-2	11-16-3		Total 35-5-3	
5			No 2 bogie					67-5-1
	No 1 bogie off tables		7-19-0	12-16-1	11-4-1		Total 31-19-2	
		10-1-0	10-7-3	11-7-3			Total 35-5-3	
6			No 2 bogie					65-2-2
		10-19-1	10-19-1	11-7-2			Total 33-6-0	

(36001 weighed at Eastleigh 31/1/50. 3,000 gallons of water, 3 tons of coal, 1 inch water in glass (cold), no coal in firebox. Weights given in tons, cwts, and quarters. *Editor's note: remember the writer states that for this weighing no 'balancing' weights were in place. Had these been so then the total weight would have been considerably greater.*)

Weight No 5 reverses the maximum and minimum side loads from those shown on weights 4 and 6 was suspect but assuming that it was worth including an average of all the weights gave the following results:

WEIGHTS	No. 1 Bogie					No. 2 Bogie
Wheel	11-3-0	11-9-0	10-15-1	10-5-2	10-15-2	11-14-1
Wheel	8-7-1	9-3-0	11-5-3	10-7-0	11-12-3	11-3-1
Axle	19-10-1	20-12-0	22-1-0	20-12-2	22-8-1	23-2-2
Total Bogie		63-3-1			66-3-1	
Total Loco			128-6-2			

Miscellaneous notes:

Valve events MN & WC. In 1948 consideration was given to altering valve events and in May No 21C104 was checked to show that a maximum cut off in foregear of 79% could be obtained. OVB directed that other locos should be altered.

Further checks made in June showed that 77% was the maximum possible giving valve openings front and back of 1-21/32' and 1-25/32' respectively. The radius rod was however riding on the bottom of the expansion link. Clearance of die block at bottom of link approx. 3/32'. Instructions were given that the 1948 interchange trial

engines and new 'West Country' Nos 34071-90 were to be fitted but apparently the alteration was also applied indiscriminately to other locos including the final batch 34091–34110. In 1951 it was reported that overtravel of piston valves necessitated increased length of steam chest liners on these altered locos but I believe no alteration was made, the cut-off reverting to 70% as designed.

Fireboxes M.N. In September 1947 it was decided by OVB that five of the third batch of ten M.N were to be fitted with welded 'U' foundation rings and five with solid rings but in 11/47 that all were to have the 'U' ring. This was not carried out.

Firebox roof stays MN & WC. In the early 1950s it had become difficult to obtain the alloy steel used for roof stays and a more normal steel was used in place. At the same time it was considered necessary to reduce boiler pressure from 280 to 250 psi.

Modified MN & WC. Although BR had produced a number of standard locos the bulk of BR services were being dealt with by locos of regional types. In 1954 it was decided that to overcome the difficulties experienced with maintenance on the MN & WC locos and in spite of their excellent performance, that all the MN and a number of the WC should be modified to have ordinary Walschaert valve gear, dispensing with the oil bath together with various other modifications including a new inside cylinder. The existing outside cylinders were retained.

'A number of modifications had been made prior to this decision but in order to ascertain how much heavier the modified locos would be it was necessary to make a careful preliminary check of weights. The locos which had received the earlier modifications were referred to as 'guinea pigs' and I give a comparison of weights.

Bulleid detail, seen here with the right-hand side of No 21C131, later No 34031. (One to please our friends who one day may be able to return the railway to the town so named.)

Merchant Navy class weights
T = tons C = Hundredweight

	Bogie		Leading		Driving		Trailing		Track		Total Eng	
	T	C	T	C	T	C	T	C	T	C	T	C
Diagram	16	14	21	0	21	0	21	0	15	1	34	15
Pre-guinea pig												
*(Second 10)	17	1	20	14	20	19	20	13	15	16	95	3
‡ 3rd 10 (35021)	17	12	20	12	21	3	20	11	15	12	95	10
*Guinea Pig	17	2	21	7	21	13	20	19	15	16	96	17

*Average weights of several locos from Eastleigh records
‡ New engine weight with stiffened front end frame showing increase of 11 cwt on the bogie, 4 cwt less on track and no change in total on coupled wheels.

	Bogie		Leading		Driving		Trailing		Track		Total Eng	
†Estimated weight of modified loco	17	7	21	12	21	19	21	4	15	16	97	18

†Included 11 cwt extra for balanced crank axle.
When modified the actual weights corresponded closely with the calculated weights.

West Country class weights
T = tons C = Hundredweight

	Bogie		Leading		Driving		Trailing		Track		Total Eng	
	T	C	T	C	T	C	T	C	T	C	T	C
Diagram	15	10	18	15	18	15	18	15	14	5	86	0
Pre-guinea pig	15	17	18	17	19	0	18	13	14	3	86	10
*Guinea Pig	16	18	19	10	91	16	19	3	14	0	88	17

*Average weights of several locos from Eastleigh records

	Bogie		Leading		Driving		Trailing		Track		Total Eng	
†Estimated weight of modified loco	16	11	19	14	20	0	19	7	14	5	89	17

†Included 11 cwt extra for balanced crank axle.
When modified the actual weights corresponded closely with the calculated weights.
(No mention is given of the identification of the actual 'guinea pig' locos'.)

[1] As there are no photographs accompanying the original piece, your editor has put together various views to provide a flavour for both the timescale and the subjects involved.

[2] Without attempting to take these few words out of context, what we have here is evidence that various senior and professional engineers were now disagreeing with the aspects of the 'Leader' design. Remember too that at the time Bulleid came to the Southern he was seen by some as a breath of fresh air, breathing life into a department that had become almost moribund. But now with his creation not performing as intended – for whatever reason – it appears to be a definite case of 'pass the buck' and ensure you are not be left taking the can for a failing project that could very well affect future career progression. Remember, Bullied was leaving and the next man in charge would want to know why and, perhaps more especially, who?

Looking north through the platforms at Blandford towards Templecombe. The signal box and down waiting shelter were located on what was in reality an island platform, although the rear of the platform was in reality fenced off at the north end. The goods shed can also be seen and whilst there were up sidings at both the south and north ends of the up platform, the majority of goods facilities were on the down side. *S. W. C. Eyers collection*

Blandford Memories

Roy White

As a boy I remember spending time at weekends — mostly during school holiday periods — waiting by the water column on the down side at Blandford station.[1] A strange place to be in the early morning, perhaps, but there was a definite ulterior motive to my intentions for about 9am the down goods from Templecombe was due and with luck I would be invited up on to the footplate where I would spend several joyous hours until dropped off again around lunchtime.

It all depended on the driver, of course, and I used to hope it would be 'Fritz' Lawrence often with his trustee steed, an old Johnson 3F, No 43194. LMS loco types then dominated the Somerset & Dorset, with the exception that is four 'West Country' Pacifics based at Bath and intended for the premier workings including, of course, the 'Pines Express'. Evidently the Pacifics were none too popular as they were later replaced by the first BR 'Standard' 5s allocated to the region, Nos 73050–2.

I well remember the exact occasion this transfer had taken place as I was playing a game of cricket on the recreation ground north of the station the railway at this point below the level of the field in a cutting. It was 4.30pm and there was the definite sound of a chime whistle. Needless to say, the cricket ceased at once and we all dashed over to fence in time to see No 73051 heading north. I was probably the keenest of the little cricketing group and for the rest of that afternoon, and indeed for years afterwards, I berated myself for having likely missed the same engine when it had, so I believed, headed south at 12.15pm, the normal southbound working for the

engine on the 4.30pm. It was only twenty-six years later that I found through one of Ivo Peters' books that No 73051 had been delivered light engine from Derby, via Willesden and Basingstoke, to Bournemouth and was only then making its way north for the first time. Certainly a long way round to reach what would be its home shed at Bath.

The time came to think of a career and the railway beckoned. I applied for a clerical position at Blandford and after what seemed an age a letter arrived enclosing a return ticket to Waterloo and an invitation to sit the clerical exam. This was followed by a trip to Eastleigh for a medical, and I was successful in both. So began my nine-year stint at Blandford, although I was not the first of my family to work on S & D, nor indeed at the same station as my half-brother, who was twelve years older than me, was already employed in the booking office. Times had also changed since my brother had started on the railway. He had to go to Bath for what was then designated 'Clerical Examination No 1'. There was a second part to be taken within two years and which included being proficient in Pitman shorthand; failure would mean you were dismissed from the service.

A few years before I started there had been two RTO NCOs based at the station, one English and one American. The reason for this was the heavy military presence in the area both at Blandford camp and the airfield at Tarrant Rushton. The British man was Bill Newman, who was originally a clerk at the station and later the station master at Templecombe.

Seen from the north end and what was the end of the single line section from Shillingstone. The necessity for the tall co-acting arm of the up starting signal can be seen here to allow a view to drivers of approaching up trains. The photo was taken from the Salisbury Road bridge (bridge No 193) taking the railway from the city of that name eventually to Shaftesbury. Behind the camera the down home signal was similarly a tall post with a co-acting arm and again to provide sighting over another overbridge. *S. W. C. Eyers collection*

The south end and viewed towards Spetisbury and Bailey Gate. Between 1919 and 1921 a connection had been provided here forming a siding to Blandford (Army) Camp. This was sited close to the end of 'down siding south', which may be discerned as the line of rails to the left of the pair of running lines. *S. W. C. Eyers collection*

Blandford was unique in two aspects so far as the S & D was concerned. First, it was the only station to be lit by electricity and, second, it was the only place to have a subway as the official means of access between the platforms.

Starting on the railway, my first task was in the goods office assisting the chief clerk. Other than dealing with the accounts he was involved with recording the movement of sacks from the West of England Sack Co. Two other clerks also assisted, one for despatches and one for receipts. Outside there was a wagon checker (to record the numbers of arriving and departing wagons), a goods porter within the goods shed, a shunter and another goods porter in the yard. All these were overseen by the station foreman, who was also responsible for the passenger side. Even so, the only time we ever saw this worthy was when the up 'Pines' was due. He would also use the (omni) 'bus phone in the booking office to report the wagon position to Bath. (The omnibus phone was an open circuit, having as its extensions the various yards and offices on its circuit. Any person could speak to anyone else but before doing so you first lifted the receiver to listen and see if it was already in use. Conservations could hardly be deemed to be private.)

On summer Saturdays when there was no scheduled goods train, the foreman would spend the morning on the platform as there was a continuous stream of northbound trains. He would also assist the signalman by taking and inserting the tablet in

the Whittaker exchange apparatus for the few trains that did not stop in the up (Shillingstone) direction. Having someone else to help certainly kept the traffic moving as the exchange apparatus was located at the south end of the up platform and the signalman would not have time to do the job himself.

We also had four road vehicles. One was a Scammell Scarab (no doubt named by the manufacture after the beetle that would scurry around seemingly busy all the time) with two trailers. Mostly this was used for large deliveries to and from the goods yard, except that is at the start and end of the school holidays at nearby Blandford school, when it was used for the collection and delivery of school luggage. This vehicle was supplemented for a time by a larger articulated unit on loan from Poole and was used in connection with the delivery of steel arriving at Blandford and destined for the pylons of a new high-tension electrical supply route then being provided across much of Dorset. Two other 3-ton covered lorries did town deliveries in the morning from the goods shed and to the more outlying locations in the afternoon. Our final vehicle was a smaller 30cwt parcels van that was engaged just on town deliveries, making two runs each day and just one on Saturdays. Even in the 1950s it was still incredible to think back and realise just how much reliance there was on the railway system for the supply of almost all the goods that were sold in the town.

Right: **The goods shed at the end of the up platform; note the two passenger platforms that, although of roughly the same length, were staggered. The school name under the nameboard may be noted. Beyond the goods shed the white end is part of the station master's house.** *S. W. C. Eyers collection*

Below: **The entrance to the goods yard off Alexandra Street, recorded late in the life of the station on 26 March 1964. Of the two sidings seen, that on the right could be used for end loading – notice the army-registered lorry – and was also accessible to the yard crane. (The crane could also reach wagons standing on the siding that ran the length of the down platform.) The siding on the left ran past the coal staithes. The large building beyond was a corn store.** *S. W. C. Eyers collection*

Below right: **A general view of the yard in 1966 with a Bedford attached to a Scammel-type trailer. The brake van is standing on the down siding with the other two sidings previously mentioned in the centre. The line past the cattle pens on the right continued on to a small coal yard.** *S. W. C. Eyers collection*

Aside from goods and parcels, there were three coal merchants in the yard. Two of these would bag and then deliver coal straight off the incoming wagons, except that is in the summer when to avoid demurrage (wagon storage) charges, the wagon was emptied and the coal taken to their own premises for storage, there being no coal pens as such in the railway goods yard. The third firm was Messrs J. Snow, a well-known coal and timber merchant that had a short siding with coal pens and an office alongside the north end of the up platform. This siding could accommodate two wagons and for 99 percent of the time was only used by wagons for the firm. The one exception was when the station's own coal supply arrived. This was then unloaded by hand on to the rear of the up platform and barrowed over to the railway's own coal store.

The timing of deliveries was crucial to the smaller firms and I well remember one of the smaller organisations, whose assets consisted of a single lorry and perhaps one or two wagons of coal a week, occasionally popping his head around the office door to enquire if there was a 'Hednesford' about? (This was the name of the colliery in Staffordshire from where he obtained most of his supplies.) We were usually able to put his mind at rest as the invoices for the arriving wagons would usually have been received earlier by passenger train.

The merchant receiving his supplies was only allowed a certain amount of time to unload his wagon, after which if it had been emptied then he should have been charged demurrage. Whether this was applied or not depended to an extent on the checker as when more wagons arrived than might otherwise be accommodated it all depended upon what was written on his record …

We had two agricultural merchants with stores in the yard, Dorset Farmers and Blandford & Webb. Both dealt with animal feed and fertilizer. Some of this was from ICI (International Chemical Industry) in the North-east and also in full train loads from Avonmouth. This latter service was one that the Western Region in its wisdom decided to re-route and so instead of its previous Avonmouth–Bath–Blandford (twenty-four-hour) routing, was instead sent from Avonmouth to Salisbury and thence to Southampton, Poole and Blandford, taking a week to arrive. Brewery traffic was also heavy and originated from Burton-on-Trent. Beer and wines were received in various size barrels destined for the local brewery, Messrs Hall & Woodhouse. After bottling where necessary these were then despatched to their various tied houses.

Smaller goods – which were the ones despatched by the railway road vans – arrived daily on the morning goods train – one van each from Nine Elms, Salisbury and Bristol. In addition there was a further van from Bournemouth (9.28pm off Poole and 10.30pm at Blandford). The contents of this van were always dealt with as the first vehicle in the morning and thus before the arrival of other three. No doubt the crew of the up night freight were glad to offload any weight they could as the night freight invariably also contained ball clay from the Isle of Purbeck destined for the potteries around Stoke-on-Trent.

At one point I was in receipt of a brake van pass, this in consequence of the need to attend a commercial improvement class every other week at Bournemouth Central. I would travel down on the 'Pines' as far as Poole before changing for a train to Central. At the conclusion of the class I made my way back to Poole and then looked for the loco that had brought the down 'Pines' earlier. This was because its return working was on this freight service, incidentally the fourth leg of its day's work and which amounted to something like 300 miles in twenty-four hours.

Riding in the gloom of the guard's brake at night I could easily see how it would be possible to doze off. Ahead you might be able to hear perhaps six wagons going over a particular rail joint, the sound getting louder and louder until the van reached the same spot. It was all very soporific and even though I was only in the van for forty-five minutes there were times when I also nearly nodded off.

Goods despatched from Blandford included 3-ton Bedford army trucks belonging to 15 RASC at Blandford Camp. This facility taught national service recruits to drive, although as these conscripts had little experience, accidents were commonplace. They were then sent to a maintenance depot at Bulwell in Nottinghamshire for repair, replacement/repaired

Looking through the station from the south. Passenger access between the platforms was via a subway. Taken in January 1966 in the very last weeks of operation, it is hard to imagine the importance the railway had played within the community. Now though there are no waiting passengers and not just due to the winter conditions. *S. W. C. Eyers collection*

A scene not so often seen, the up side exterior accessed off what was Oakfield Street. *S. W. C. Eyers collection*

vehicles returning by train the same way. Sugar beet was also despatched to the factory at Kidderminster, the amount that was allowed to be sent closely controlled via a system of permits. In return we received what was a very smelly pulp intended as cattle feed, or the less smelly and easier to handle similar product this time compressed in the form of nuts.

Wattle hurdles was another traffic – wattles were made from hazel that had been coppiced. This would be collected by the Scammel and might be in small consignments, in which case it was dealt with through the goods shed, or even as much as full wagon loads.

Further traffic came from a firm of agricultural engineers who produced pig huts with a semicircular roof – almost a miniaturised version of a Nissen hut. These were charged at full wagon rates as, although light in weight, it was only possible to fit two in a standard open wagon, whilst they also had to be loaded using the crane. The same firm also produced various animal feeders as well as farm gates.

Worth mentioning is that Blandford had its own goods service and was not subject to the vagaries of the pick-up goods as applied to many of the other stations where there was less traffic. This train arrived from the direction of Templecombe.

As wagons arrived, so the station foreman would remove the wagon labels from one side the other label remaining in place for identification by the consignee. The majority of the train was quickly shunted over to the up platform whilst the loco propelled the three road vans (those from Nine Elms, Salisbury and Bristol) to a shunting neck north of the station and where once uncoupled the goods checker would run them down to the goods shed by gravity. The remainder of the train was then moved into the shunting neck at the south end of the station. As the goods might consist of up to thirty wagons this could cause problems purely on the basis of space and was made especially difficult as the timetable indicated a passenger crossing taking place between 9.45 and 9.57am – the up train always arriving first.

Once the passenger services had departed the goods returned to the down line. Its formation included a brake van front and rear, and shunting could now commence. Following the passage of the up 'Pines' at 10.20am, the front brake van was moved across to the up platform and its brakes screwed hard on. Any empty or full wagons for despatch were now shunted over against the barked van and coupled. In this way the train was slowly made up ready for departure at 1.16pm.

In the meanwhile more manoeuvring would be required later as both platforms had again to be cleared by midday to permit up and down passenger trains to cross between 12.15 and 12.30pm.

After a year in the goods office I moved over to the passenger side for further training and initially working a day shift. The staff consisted of the station master and two booking clerks, who worked either 7.30am to 2.30pm or 1pm to 8pm over six days. A third clerk worked a day shift from 8.30am to 4.30pm with a one-hour lunch break at 12pm. He then caught the 1.13pm train to Bailey Gate, where he dealt with the paperwork for the milk traffic from the United Dairies depot to London. The volume of this could vary from nothing at all to up to four tanks a day dependent upon the time of year. It was said the same factory housed the largest cheese factory in the country at the time, possibly even in the world.

Watercress was another traffic from Bailey Gate, with large quantities sent out on weekdays for which purpose two bogie vans were attached to the rear of the 3.40pm ex Bournemouth West, this service also being known as the 'Up Mail'. This train was shown in the timetable as having priority over all other workings as it had to connect at Mangotsfield with the Bristol to Newcastle mail train. On occasions there was so much watercress that further punnets were loaded into the front and rear guard's compartments of what was the regular three-coach Maunsell passenger set. The clerk also returned to Blandford on this train.

The down goods train in the platform. The starting signal will be seen be at 'on', indicating the engine may well be involved in shunting the yard. On the extreme right is the very short up siding. Note too the mail bags on the platform trolley awaiting loading. *S. W. C. Eyers collection*

The remainder of the staff consisted one porter and one junior porter on early and late shift: 7am to 3pm and 2pm to 10pm. There were also two signalmen, ostensibly on '6–2' and '2–10' shifts, although the early turn man started before 6am as the down mail was due at 6.05am and he had to open the gates to the goods yard so the local postman could collect bags of mail off this train. The late turn man similarly had overtime at the end of his shift as it was 10.38pm before the 9.28pm freight cleared Shillingstone and 'Train out of section' would be received.

The two junior porters included among their duties responsibility for the signal lamps. It was quite a walk to the up and down distant signals and, of course, they were at totally opposite ends of the station. They also had to climb the up starting signal, a very tall post with a co-acting arm required for sighting purposes over the top of the station canopy.

Other staff included a signal linesman and a telegraph linesman, although both of these individuals took care not just of the immediate station area. There was also a permanent way gang who, with responsibility for six route miles, were also issued with a Wickham-type trolley.

After a time one of the regular shift clerks took a position on the relief staff and I took his place. There were also some changes to the working hours on Saturday that meant the late turn man now started at noon instead of 1pm. This was to allow the early turn man time to get home and then return to catch the 1.13pm train if he wished and so reach Bournemouth. Otherwise the next down train would have been the 4.50pm down 'Pines'. Saturday late turn was also when the booking clerk did the payroll for the week, a task that took most of his shift. In the summer he was also required to be at the station from 10am until 1pm so there was always the opportunity to finish it then as otherwise a summer Saturday could be a busy time.

We still had a lot of military passenger traffic due to national service. Although my friends were called up, somehow I managed to escape; perhaps it was something to do with having a surname towards the end of the alphabet.

There were four different Army units at Blandford, all of which might require tickets in advance when going on leave or moving to other units. Fridays were particularly busy as there were individuals going home on forty-eight-hour passes. Unfortunately we could only issue a single to these men as there was no suitable Sunday return and instead they had to return to Salisbury and either make their own way from there or use Army transport provided. Fortunately a list of tickets required was passed to us in advance often for travel up to a week ahead. As such we would have an idea of the number of men travelling and if necessary could order extra carriages from Bournemouth. They virtually all went north as the best London service was then via Templecombe.

Further special traffic came from any of the four public schools in the area but again we were given notice of required destinations in advance, sometimes unusual places – thank goodness for our most comprehensive fares book! The Blandford schools traffic could warrant a special train to Waterloo and extra carriages to a northbound service. Luggage was collected by railway lorry from three of the schools and brought to the station. Bryanston involved the most traffic, so much so that two clerks and two porters would spend the whole day at the school whilst the Scammel shuttled to and fro with luggage usually making four round trips. The final lorry journey involved the four-wheeler, which would collect any final items of luggage plus the staff and the paperwork generated. School luggage, trunks and tuck boxes caused more strained backs than almost any other goods as two identical-looking trunks could be so different, one appearing to be almost nailed to the ground and the next the opposite.

The return luggage arriving was spread over about a week. Virtually every down train would have some items, which were then stored under cover in the down side waiting room until there was enough for a full load to the particular school. The porter would call out the details of each trunk and these were entered on separate loading sheets for each school. I recall working on this job after the Christmas holidays in fog so thick I couldn't see the porter who was calling out the consignment details!

The up side building replete with the contemporary signage and posters of the day, 20 March 1964.
S. W. C. Eyers collection

At Blandford the booking and parcels plus a store occupied one large room on the up side. There were two booking office windows on one end and facing the main waiting room. A parcels counter effectively divided the room in half, the whole heated by a tortoise stove that at times would glow red.

After the early turn booking clerk had gone home it was the job of the late turn man to deal with all tickets and parcels plus telephone enquiries.

Tarrant Rushton airfield had been relinquished by the RAF soon after the Second World War and was taken over by Alan Cobham and his firm, Flight Refuelling. The same company was involved in the manufacture of aircraft components and packages would arrive in a van about 9.30am, all intended to travel north of the 'Pines'. It was the ideal train for this as it had so many connections in the Midlands and beyond. As an example, items for Sheffield would be loaded into a van at the front, which was in turn attached to the 'Devonian' at Birmingham. Other through vehicles would allow passage to Liverpool, Leeds or Bradford, with the main part of the 'Pines', of course, continuing to Manchester. All this would cease when the through trains were discontinued in 1962.

Although it has been mentioned elsewhere, it is still worth reiterating the vast amount of traffic in the form of through trains that would use the line on summer Saturdays. These consisted no fewer than eighteen southbound workings, all from distant destinations and including four overnight workings. All of these would stop at Blandford, and even more traffic on occasions when further trains were run in connection with wakes weeks, so called as this was the times the northern factories would shut down for the annual holiday.

Of course, what goes one way must go the other and there would be a similar number of northbound workings later in the day, this time not all stopping at Blandford. It was also the only time when the tablet pick-up apparatus at the south of the station was used. Should there be a miss then the train still had time to stop before reaching the single line. By comparison, down trains leaving the single line would deposit the tablet at the catcher at the north end of the down platform, Blandford being the start of the double line south as far as Corfe Mullen.

I mentioned the volume and general variety of traffic the railway handled earlier, indeed enough to keep our three vans busy. Lyon's cakes – always on a Thursday and seemingly enough for a box to almost every shop in the area – mail order catalogue goods, groceries, general provisions, drapery; almost everything that was sold in the shops. Regular visitors would include the two town fishmongers who every day would be waiting for the first down train ready to collect their fish that had been sent from Hull or Grimsby.

We also handled livestock, day-old chicks both in and out, dogs, calves, these in a sack with just their head and legs sticking through, pigs, cavies (another name for guinea pigs) and Dorset horn rams 'on the hoof'. A quirk with the latter was that they had to be weighed, which involved turning the

Busy times. 4F No 44422 has steam to spare as it awaits departure with a Bournemouth West to Bristol service, *S. W. C. Eyers collection*

No 73049 seen again in the down direction and arriving from the north, 26 March 1964. *S. W. C. Eyers collection*

In the opposite direction, sister engine No 73051 leaves with the 9.40am Bournemouth West to Templecombe, 26 March 1964. *S. W. C. Eyers collection*

This time it is the turn of a Class 4 tank engine to take centre stage at the up platform and in charge of a short working to Templecombe, 11 January 1966. *vS. W. C. Eyers collection*

The tablet apparatus at the down end of the up platform. Alongside is one of the famed S & D trespass notices, many of which survived until the very end and are now prized items. *S. W. C. Eyers collection*

animal on its back on the weighing machine. The fun really started when the ram was loaded in the guard's van and could involve up to four people including the guard, although if this was not enough the loco fireman might be persuaded to assist.

I recall once when a Stilton cheese arrived consigned to a particular grocer but he refused to accept it as it was cracked. Usually when this happened we were told to send the damaged item to Waterloo for the manager's restaurant, although this time we were instead instructed to 'sell to best advantage' and so offset the claim. We sold pieces to anyone who wanted any, and not just railway staff although the booking office did smell somewhat for weeks afterwards. Another product was mushrooms, large quantities being loaded on the 3.40pm from Bournemouth. Again it was all hands to get the goods away on time.

The down platform at Blandford would only accommodate eight coaches and this was inconvenient when the down 'Pines' arrived as, having twelve vehicles, it meant the last four were off the platform. On these occasions the booking office was locked and the clerk went out to assist with visibility as at least two people plus the guard would be needed to safely ensure the train could draw forward on the curved platform. It was all part of the service and to ensure that any passengers wishing to alight from the rear four coaches could do so with ease. It also enabled us to unload any parcels in the Liverpool

and Sheffield brake vans as failure to do so would have meant these goods going further south to Bournemouth and likely as not otherwise arriving back with us until the next morning.

I recall one evening when the 6.40pm arrived from Bournemouth and a lady leant out of the compartment to enquire if she was on the right train for Dorchester? When we told her 'No' she complained that she had seen this destination on the engine. It transpired she had got on at Poole but should have joined the one after the S & D service. Luckily at that time there was still an hourly Wilts & Dorset bus service from Salisbury to Weymouth via Blandford and Dorchester, and a bit of railway goodwill was recovered by getting the junior porter to assist her to where she could join the next bus.

To someone who had seen the S & D in its heyday is was soul destroying to watch what happened towards the end. Trains retimed to deliberately miss connections at Templecombe, the end of the through trains of course, and all our traffic deliberately rerouted so as to make it difficult if not impossible to maintain the one we had once provided. Come 1966 and almost everyone was made redundant, except that is for the shunter and goods checker, dealing with wagon load goods only. Instead of through services the railway was now worked as a long siding from Broadstone as far as Blandford. Beyond us the route was simply abandoned, any parcels and freight smalls being handled from Poole. Bailey Gate finally closed as a railway milk depot in 1969 and with it came the true end of the S & D.

and to follow …

[1] The name was changed to 'Blandford Forum' in 1953.

The Blandford station St John's Ambulance team seen here taking part in a competition at Yeovil. From left to right they are: Examining doctor; Sidney Cox, station master at Sturminster Newton; Bert Scammell, signalman at Shillingstone; Roy White, clerk at Blandford (who is examining the patient's arm); and Pat Holmes, junior porter at Blandford. *Roy White collection*

Trolleys on the S & D

Jeffery Grayer

J effery recalls the humble permanent way ganger's trolley, so often overlooked when it comes to railway photography.

A number of such trolleys operated on the S & D including No B11W, which was stabled in a trolley shed at Midsomer Norton South station, in a shed just to the north of Silver Street overbridge. B31W was photographed in a bay at Shepton Mallet's Charlton Road station in May 1964. B29W was to be

In this view dating from the early 1960s an unidentified Wickham is seen passing 'Midford A' ground frame, which controlled access to Midford's small goods yard. The line branching off to the right led to the yard, which contained a crane, a small shed and a couple of sidings. Situated as it was on a shelf on the hillside, there was no room for a goods yard at the station itself, hence one was provided some distance to the north. It was closed in June 1963 with the track being removed a year later in June 1964. The ground frame was released by the section tablet from Midford signal box.

found parked on the centre road, formerly used by Mendip banking locomotives, at Evercreech Junction during the process of track recovery following closure of the line in March 1966. It remained there, latterly minus one axle, until the recovery railhead reached the Junction in February 1968, when it was recovered by road. In February 2017 trolley No B40W, was delivered to the S & D preservation society at Midsomer Norton for restoration. Built in 1956, its allocations included Oxford, AfonWen, Borth, Machynlleth and Aberystwyth. Sold out of BR service to a quarry, it found its way to the Battlefield Railway at Shackerstone in Leicestershire in 1991. It will make a welcome addition to the society's fleet.

Above: **Taken on 9 July 1967, incidentally the last day of SR steam, this view of the deserted station at Evercreech Junction shows the permanent way trolley B29W parked in the centre road, the former haunt of banking locomotives.**

Left: **Another view on the same day looking south again shows the PW trolley, which at this time appears to have both axles intact.**

(This pair of images can be found in Jeff's latest book on the S & D, *Impermanent Ways Special No. 1.*)

An autumn 1967 view reveals the trolley parked by the buffer stop on the centre road. Shortly after this it lost one of its axles and would remain here until February of the following year, when it was removed by road. Various rail vehicles with recovered materials abound. *John Lakey*

British Railways Southern Region Magazine

Michael Upton

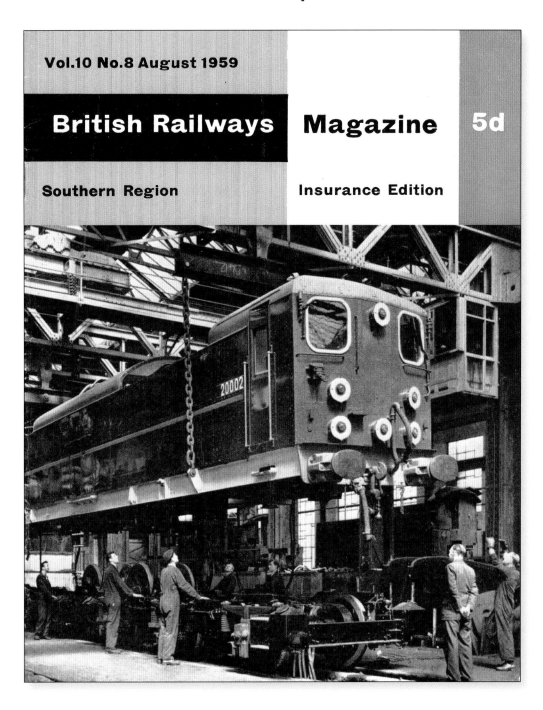

Vol.10 No.8 August 1959

British Railways **Magazine** 5d

Southern Region **Insurance Edition**

As a resource to the historian, the BR(S) magazine is a valued and yet often overlooked source of material.

I t has sometimes been common in the past to dismiss this and the other regional BR magazines, but the railways did not suddenly stop at midnight at the end of December 1947, they continued, initially unaltered and with change taking place slowly – exactly as they had post-grouping and indeed in the same way years later post-privatisation.

Consequently, for more than a decade the magazine continued to applaud the various achievements of the region, as witness some of the following examples taken directly from its pages.

March 1950: Award for Bravery

Motorman Bishop was driving his train into Angmering station when a lady dropped from the platform onto the track in front of it. Unable to stop until the leading bogie had passed over the lady, Motorman Bishop went back, squeezed himself down onto the track and prevented her from sustaining a fatal injury by contact with the conductor rail.

Development at Fawley

Work on the Anglo American Oil Company new oil refinery at Fawley is now in full swing, and ever increasing quantities of materials are being received at frequent intervals in Southampton Docks. The articles of equipment landed from the freighter 'Vandalia' on 3rd January included a 45 ton diesel locomotive which will be used inside the company's new Esso Cadland sidings. Although the construction of the engine gave cause for some anxiety on a question of clearance with bridges etc during its haul to Fawley by rail, the journey was affected safely on 5th January, under special working arrangements.

The Railway Was Not To Blame

Recently a notice appeared on the screen of a Worthing cinema informing patrons that the full programme would not be shown as advertised owing to the film being delayed on rail.

On learning of the incident, the Station Master immediately got in touch with the manager of the cinema, informing him he had received no such complaint and offering assistance. The manager admitted the incident was not the fault of the railway, as the film had been dispatched in error to a town in Norfolk. He apologised and withdrew the notice.

Vol. 11   No. 6   June 1960   **SOUTHERN** EDITION
BRITISH RAILWAYS **MAGAZINE**

Regional Editorial Offices: Waterloo Station, London Waterloo 5151, Ext. 2062
Advertisement Offices: R. Harris Publications Ltd, 39 Hertford Street, London W1 Grosvenor 3877

The last of his line

John Henry Bastin, toll collector at Langstone Bridge, Hants, receives a long service certificate from district traffic superintendent Mr. H. E. Barber, on the day he retired.

April 1950: Goodbye to Aquitania

On 19 February the Cunard liner *Aquitania* left Southampton on her last voyage. She was bound for Clyde and the breakers yard to be broken up for scrap. A she passed the British Railways Signal Station at the New Docks for the last time, a flag signal bid her 'goodbye with regret.'

July 1951: Casualties in Korea

Among the casualties sustained by the gallant Gloucesters in Korea are two SR men, and the sympathies of readers is extended to the relatives in their sorrow. *There follows in the magazine the details of an engine cleaner at Eastleigh and a goods porter at Bricklayers Arms who sadly lost their lives.*

October 1950: 2,500 Children Travel by Southern Electric to the Sea

On August 24 three special electric corridor trains left St Helier station with nearly 2,500 children bound for a day by the sea at Littlehampton.

The Mother, the Baby, and the Railways Staff

A baby was the central figure in an incident at Redhill recently, when the willing service of railway staff earned the grateful thanks of a distraught mother. Here is the story in a nutshell.

On a late Brighton to Victoria train during the return August bank holiday traffic, a mother with one child left the train at Redhill to use the station lavatory, leaving in the train her handbag and a sleeping four-year-old baby. The train departed before the mother returned.

The mother immediately told the station inspector what had happened, and he telephoned control, the understanding being that the mother and one child would be on the following train for Victoria.

Police, Croydon and Clapham Junction stations were communicated with, and news was received that the baby, still asleep, had been handed to the staff at East Croydon. Before the following train left Redhill the anxious mother was informed that her baby would be handed to her at East Croydon, together with her handbag, and the two little handbags belonging to the children.

August 1951: Orpington – Day-Old Chick Traffic

Headcorn handles a great deal of this traffic. The tiny birds arrive in specially made cardboard boxes which go to all parts of the country. Some even go to South Africa and Australia via Charing Cross and London Airport.

Mr Wills the station master at Headcorn has received the following letter from Sterling Poultry Products Ltd of Biddenden, one of the principal consigners of this class of traffic:

Now that our busy season for this traffic has come to an end, may we take the opportunity of thanking you and your staff for the fine co-operation you have given us. Something like 250,000 day old chicks must have passed through your hands in the last 12 months and we very much appreciate the speed with which they were dispatched.

That is a lot of day-old chicks from one station. My grandparents kept chicken and I recall my grandfather collecting the occasional box of day-old chicks from the station staff at Bramley for Silchester, having been offloaded from the guard's van on a Reading to Basingstoke working. I think the day-old requirement is significant as after that time the chicks need to be fed and watered, while for the first twenty-four hours they can survive alone. In that issue there was also a piece on the new ship MV Shanklin for the IOW service, I remember travelling on that ship many times. Also, an article on the New Golden Arrow, oil traffic on the Isle of Grain branch and palletisation of freight on BR.

May 1954: Farm Removal

Mr D Penrose chose to move his farm from Northallerton to Witley by rail. Upon arrival at Witley the Surrey advertiser reports him saying, 'it was by far the cheapest way of getting all my stuff here.'

The special train which comprised of 15 vehicles, not forgetting Gyp the sheepdog, Peggy the horse and five cats, left Northallerton at 5.20pm on March 25th, and travelled via Banbury and Reading, arriving on time at Witley at 4.28am the following morning.

The household furniture, which was conveyed in two containers, was detached at Guildford for delivery by road to Hazelbrook Farm. It is understood that Mr and Mrs Penrose and their three children appreciated the cups of tea thoughtfully provided by Mr H Foxlow, Station Master, Witley, upon their arrival.

June 1954

A follow-on letter from Mr W. Neal re an article about the first woman railway clerk:

In the 1880s say up to 1885, Miss Nellie Piggot was booking clerk at Ockley, her father being station master. On his death, she left and went to Brighton where she was employed by the Post Office. In 1890 I was a learner at Ockley, and having passed the telegraph test relieved the booking clerks at Ockley, Holmwood and Leatherhead and was appointed telegraph clerk at Horsham in 1891. At that time there were several woman clerks in the district served by the transmitting office, Miss Harris from Partridge Green, Miss Piper from Bramley as booking clerks and Miss Bishop as telegraph clerk at Sutton. I believe there were several others but cannot bring them to mind at the moment. I would also mention that during the first

world war, Miss Edie Shepperd was booking clerk at Ockley, her father being station master there. After about a year, she was appointed Station Mistress at Ardingly, the only one I believe, ever to be appointed.

From the Courtesy Column

Letter from a watercress producer to the station master at Bailey Gate:

Credit must be given to the service of British Railways. Obviously, such a perishable product must go by passenger train, and the 4.15pm from Bailey Gate ensures early arrival at all the Northern and Midland markets early the following morning, even allowing for the transhipment at Birmingham. Breaking down the bulk consignment in the truck is made easy by the use of different and distinctive coloured labels for each salesman.

Oct 1954: Norwood Yard – Theft of Coal

Goods guard J K Wood Norwood Yard was recently seen by Mr J Bridger District Traffic Superintendent, and presented with a voucher in recognition of his alertness which led to the apprehension of the person responsible for the theft of a *truck of coal*. Guard Wood was working a freight train and observed a label was removed and the wagon shunted into another firm's siding on route.

Vol. 11   No. 7   July, 1960

SOUTHERN EDITION
BRITISH RAILWAYS **MAGAZINE**

Regional Editorial Offices, Waterloo Station, London Waterloo 5151, Ext. 2062

Advertisement Offices: R. Harris Publications Ltd, 39 Hertford Street, London W1 Grosvenor 3877

An apple for the driver

Attractive Miss J. Webster of Hobart offers an apple to Driver W. Clissold, of Salisbury, at Waterloo on 17 May (see story on page 192)

Out of Gauge Loads at Hook

Arrangements were recently made with the London Midland and Western Regions for four steel girders 128ft long. 10ft 4½ inches high and 2ft wide weighing 45 ton each to be conveyed from Butterley (LMR) to Hook (SR) via Leamington and Reading in connection with the construction of a new bridge over the Western section of line on this region at Blackbridge approximately quarter of a mile west of Hook station.

These girders passed two at a time by special train loaded on the LMR girder wagons MA, producing a maximum height of 13ft 6½ inches. This is outside the loading gauge and by reason of this and their length, movement was subject to heavy restrictions, particularly when negotiating crossovers and junctions, and when passing under bridges.

The girders were erected by the contractors Caffin and Co Ltd, under engineer's possession on the night of May 29/30 (the late Spring bank holiday) using the Willesden LMR 50 ton Motive Power Steam crane.

An LMR crane – I wonder why the SR did not provide one?

October 1955: Hop Picking

Despite the mechanical age and the introduction of hop picking machines, the exodus of many thousands of Londoners to the Kent hop gardens began on August 27th, when the first of several 'hop picking specials' left London for the Weald of Kent.

This season's crop, rated one of the best ever, is expected to be a record. At the peak of the season it is anticipated over 25,000 hop pickers friends will have made the annual pilgrimage at weekends, resulting in the running of approximately 90 special trains outward and return.

This was only the weekend traffic, what about the trains to take the hop pickers who were staying in the area for the whole hop picking season? Ninety trains for just their friends at the weekend? Interesting …

December 1955: A Letter of Thanks

I use the Folkestone trains pretty frequently, and I feel I should write to you and let you know the consistent spirit of enterprise which is being shown by your drivers and fireman on these services.

Last Saturday I went down on the 12.55pm 80 minutes train to Folkestone Central. Conditions as far as Knockholt were not entirely favourable, with quite a lot of wet leaves drifting onto the track, and to make matters worse we had a distant signal check outside Knockholt. This as you know is the worst part of the climb. Most unexpectedly we had another distant against us at Smeeth. Notwithstanding these severe checks we made arrival at Folkestone Central one minute early. This meant, as far as I can estimate, a net time of 76 minutes from Charing Cross.

I was so impressed I got the name of the driver and fireman on arrival at Folkestone. The drivers name is Kirk and the fireman Willis. They are both Ramsgate men.

I would be most grateful if you will be so very kind as to convey to the authorities my appreciation of the excellent work shown by the crew of the 12.55, which was more than in keeping with the finest traditions of the old Southern.

My return trip was equally as good, and as the gentleman in my compartment remarked to me, this type of running makes so much difference to business men who want to keep their appointments in time.

March 1956: 'New Look' Engine Now in Service

Modifications have now been completed to the Merchant Navy class locomotive No 35018 British India Line, which is the first of 30 engines of this class to be altered to *improve further their performance (my italics!)*. While they have given sterling service and have demonstrated their ability to run to time, the present alterations will result in reduced operating and maintenance costs. The alterations were carried out mainly in the locomotive works at Eastleigh, and have resulted in a considerable change to the locomotives' appearance.

The Merchant Navy class engines were first introduced on the Southern Railway in 1941, and have hauled the heaviest and fastest trains on the Southern main line to Bournemouth and the West of England, as well as many of the boat trains to the channel ports.

August 1959: Cake

To mark the end of steam trains from London to the Kent coast, Mrs Dorothy Talkington *(can that surname be real!)* of Birchington baked a cake and presented it to the local Station Master.

When the last 'steamer' came down on Sunday night, 14th June, Station Master Mr B. S. Bellingham offered a slice each to driver, fireman and guard. And he also gave them a glass of champagne. *(No drugs and alcohol policy in those days)*

Outsize Train

A copy of the Daily Sketch dated 5th April 1915 in which the following appears:

The first excursion train to Brighton less than eighty years ago started at London Bridge at 9am with 45 carriages and 4 engines. At New Cross and Croydon the train picked up 12 more carriages and 2 engines. A contemporary chronicler reported that the greatest apprehension prevailed at Brighton station until 1.30pm, when the monster train of 57 carriages and 6 engines steamed safely into the terminus.

Was this journalist licence or did a train of that length really arrive at Brighton?

Michael concludes:

I have likely taken up too much of your time and now I have to round off this random section of snippets from the staff magazine. I do hope you have enjoyed reading and I have also attached a few scans from various copies, you might find them interesting too: the Spotlight on Droxford from the back cover, each month a different station/the front cover of August 1959 shows No 20002 at Eastleigh, with the caption reading:

LOWER AWAY! and several pairs of young eyes look anxiously as the body of giant Co-Co electric locomotive starts to be lowered onto its bogies. The locomotive has just been overhauled at Eastleigh works; and this is one of the many jobs in which the apprentices 'our craftsman of tomorrow,' give a hand.

Photograph and accompanying story about the ganger and the baby rabbits at Shawford – note a train approaching on the down line! Who would have thought the SR employed the toll collector for Langston Road Toll Bridge. And not forgetting the attractive Miss Webster offering a basket of apples to the driver of the Merchant Navy. She is on the trackside at Waterloo, not a bit of PPE and certainly no safety boots! Wonderful stuff.

SPOTLIGHT

DROXFORD

ONE Friday afternoon in June, 1944, a special train slid quietly into a siding at DROXFORD station, 63¼ miles from Waterloo on the Alton-Fareham branch, or more familiarly, the Meon Valley line.

Thus started two notable days in the life of DROXFORD, for the special train was the Prime Minister's, and its presence at this small Hampshire station was in connection with no less event than the landing on the Normandy beaches of the Allied forces. In addition to the Prime Minister there were at DROXFORD at some time during those momentous days Mr. Mackenzie King, Mr. Peter Fraser, Sir G. Huggins, General Smuts, General Eisenhower, General de Gaulle, Mr. Anthony Eden, Mr. Ernest Bevin and Air Marshal Tedder. The village says that it was here that the decision to postpone "Overlord" (the codeword for the invasion) was taken.

Thus was history made at DROXFORD—the home, incidentally, of Captain Warburton Lee of Narvik fame, the first V.C. of the Second World War.

To-day DROXFORD deals mainly with people and things agricultural. Of the present staff only Signalman Gould of those depicted was working at the station through the "D-day" period. Our photographs are of Messrs. W. E. Squire, Station Master, Wickham, i/c DROXFORD; R. Daniels, Senior Porter, who looks after all the office work; R. Gould and H. Dudman, Signalmen.

Exeter to Plymouth in Steam

Alan Postlethwaite

Built from 1823 to a gauge of 4ft 6in, the horse-drawn Plymouth & Dartmoor Railway opened in stages to Princetown. Its terminus was at Sutton Harbour with a branch to Cattewater. The SDR/GWR subsequently worked the Sutton branch in broad gauge while the L&SWR/SR worked Cattewater in standard gauge. Both were freight only:

The L&SWR reached Exeter in 1860, sixteen years after the Bristol & Exeter and some 90ft more elevated. To reach the rest of Devon and Cornwall, the L&SWR built the Exeter bank with a gradient of 1 in 37 down to St Davids. Various banking engines were used to assist heavy up trains on the bank. This is class E1/R tank No 32697. *© Bluebell, CH 1957*

At Exeter St Davids, class T9 No 30717 blows off while waiting to climb the Exeter bank. *© Bluebell, CH 1957*

Between banking duties, class Z No 30952 tops up with water and tea at Exeter Central. © *Bluebell, AFP 1959*

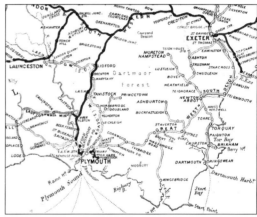

A section of *Airey's Railway Map of England & Wales*, published by McCorquodale in 1893.

Class T9 No 30717 brings a Plymouth to Exeter train into Okehampton. The main line to Plymouth was double track, whereas its withered branches to the north coast were single track with passing stations.
© *Bluebell, CH 1957*

At Cowley Bridge Junction, class N No 31838 brings an Ilfracombe train off the L&SWR on to the GWR main line. When the River Exe flooded here, alternative routes from Plymouth to London were via Totnes, St Davids and Exeter Central or (in theory at least) a long detour via Yeoford, Barnstaple and Taunton. But was the latter ever used? © *Bluebell, CH 1957*

Dwarfed by Dartmoor near Okehampton, a Light Pacific heads an up freight. *AFP 1959*

Built in 1885, class 0495 No 30581 simmers gently at Okehampton MPD. *JJS 1950*

Class WC No 34029 *Lundy* crosses Meldon viaduct with a train to Padstow. *CH 1957*

Between Lydford and Tavistock, the L&SWR and GWR lines ran parallel. The L&SWR's Brentor station was built to main line standards. Just passing is Prairie tank No 4555 with a Launceston to Plymouth train. © Bluebell, JJS 1962

Near Bere Alston, thirty-four years after the grouping, a vintage L&SWR train is headed by class O2 tank No 30193 on a Tavistock service. The main line closed in 1968 between Meldon quarry and Bere Alston. © Bluebell, CH 1957

A Light Pacific heads a train across the graceful Tavy viaduct, part steel truss and part stone arch. © Bluebell, AFP 1959

Right: **At Bere Alston, girls are in full-skirted dresses and a National Serviceman is hand-in-hand with his sweetheart – just. Activity on the up platform is pell-mell with the arrival of a smart Maunsell train to Exeter.** *© Bluebell, AFP 1959*

Below: **An up train on the all-steel Tamerton viaduct. Tamerton Foliot station is in the distant cutting.** *© Bluebell, AFP 1959*

Headed by D2176, an up freight passes through St Budeaux (Victoria Road). The down starting signals are: L&SWR Main Line (left), GWR Main Line (centre) and an industrial branch (right). This connection to the GWR gave the L&SWR access to the RN Dockyard at Devonport. In 1964, the L&SWR main line closed between here and Devonport Junction. The line north to Bere Alston remains open to this day for Gunnislake trains. © Bluebell, JJS 1962

In a scene reminiscent of Chatham, class WC No 34108 *Wincanton* enters Ford with an up train. © Terry Nicholls 1963

Dissatisfied with the standards of service provided by the GWR, the Plymouth Devonport & South Western Junction Railway was founded by local businessmen to connect the L&SWR with Plymouth from Tavistock. The PD&SWJR also built the branch from Bere Alston to Callington. Devonport (Kings Road) was the original L&SWR terminus with trains arriving from the east. The main building and most of the facilities were therefore on the on the north platform, seen here. When the PD&SWJR opened in 1890, trains arrived instead from the west and this station ceased to be a terminus. © Bruce Hunt collection

The great overall roof of Devonport (Kings Road) was destroyed by bombing in 1941. The former L&SWR engine shed is on the right. The branch to Stonehouse Ocean Quay descends steeply into a tunnel under the goods shed. Express passenger services ran between Ocean Quay and Waterloo from 1904 until 1911. The Stonehouse Pool branch remained open for freight until 1966. The train here is a cross-country service to Portsmouth and Brighton. © *Alistair Jeffory collection 1964*

Plymouth North Road station was rebuilt during 1958–62. Its style was functional rather than photogenic, so an interesting train was often an essential component of a good photo. Here, class M7 No 30036 is pulling out with empty stock of the 17.30 service from Brentor. It comprises one Maunsell coach and a Bulleid set. Victorian terraced housing in pastels contrasts with the tall grey BR office block, Intercity House, under construction beyond. © *Bernard Mills, 1961*

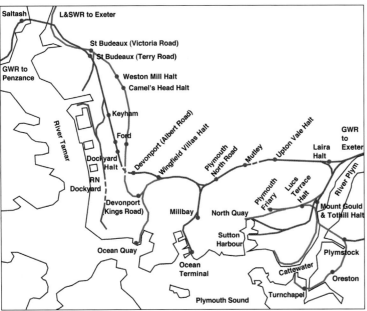

Although Plymouth North Road was joint, the Great Western always seemed dominant. Even for a Southern diehard, it was impossible not to recognise and admire its presence. Here is a tribute to GWR main line steam. Bound for Penzance, No 7006 *Lydford Castle* restarts while another 4-6-0 makes smoke on the Millbay line. *Bluebell, AFP 1959*

Photographed from Lucas Terrace Halt, class WC No 34023 *Blackmore Vale* brings empty stock from North Road to Plymouth Friary. The branch to Turnchapel and Cattewater rises on the right. Friary MPD is behind the camera on the right. *Bluebell, AFP 1959*

Its steel roof trusses set upon brick walls, Friary engine shed had generous glazing. On shed in the smoky cavern are PD&SWJR 0-6-2 tank No 30758 *Lord St Levan*, a B4 tank and L&SWR class O2 tank No 30207. © Bluebell, JJS 1950

When the PD&SWJR opened in 1890, L&SWR main line trains arriving from the west terminated temporarily at North Road. The L&SWR needed a new terminus further east and the result was Plymouth Friary. This opened in 1891 on the site of an earlier goods station. In this iconic view from L&SWR days, class O2 tank No 233 is in the up bay alongside a delightful wooden signal bracket with slender starting arms. The 'B' signal box is an L&SWR type 3b on a brick base. Beyond the carriage sidings to the left are the goods yard and the short goods branch to North Quay.
© Lens of Sutton

Plymouth Friary MPD opened in 1908, replacing a smaller MPD next to Friary goods shed. The three-road through shed is to the same design as the one at Basingstoke. Three class M7 tanks stand at the east end. The third road was used by ash wagons. The coaling siding is on the left and the turntable is behind the camera, alas too short for Light Pacifics, which had to turn on the Mount Gould triangle. The shear legs (far left) span a short siding by the workshop.
© Roger Griffiths collection 1954

The architecture of Friary station had the restful air of a country mansion. A nice finishing touch on the departure side was the forecourt canopy. The station closed to passengers in 1958 to become a freight and empty stock depot. Our outward journey is now complete except for excursions over the local SR branch lines that follow. © Bluebell, AFP 1959

Class B4 No 30088 at work on the Cattewater branch. *© Bluebell, AFP 1959*

From Cattewater Junction, the line to Plymstock crosses the River Plym on Laira Bridge while the Cattewater branch descends on the right. The locomotive is D2177. *© Bluebell, JJS 1962*

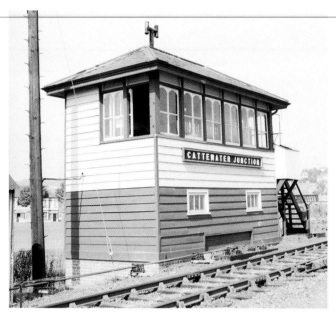

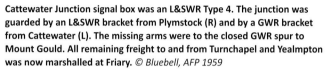

Cattewater Junction signal box was an L&SWR Type 4. The junction was guarded by an L&SWR bracket from Plymstock (R) and by a GWR bracket from Cattewater (L). The missing arms were to the closed GWR spur to Mount Gould. All remaining freight to and from Turnchapel and Yealmpton was now marshalled at Friary. © Bluebell, AFP 1959

The L&SWR's single line over Laira Bridge opened in 1892 to Plymstock and was extended to Turnchapel in 1897. When the GWR opened its branch to Yealmpton in 1898, Plymstock became a Y-junction station with two sides. In the L&SWR platform, class O2 tank No 30182 arrives with a set of gate stock to Turnchapel. Just beyond, Pannier tank No 4693 stands on the L&SWR freight line. Coal shovelling is in progress in a most basic of goods yards. © Bluebell, JJS 1950

Some forty strong, a boys' band is assembled on the L&SWR platform at Plymstock. The signal at danger suggests that their destination was in the Plymouth direction. Were they changing trains between the GWR and L&SWR? And was this train a special? Plymstock's station buildings were destroyed by bombing in 1941 and were replaced by primitive huts. The only canopy had been on the GWR platform to the left of this scene. The Yealmpton branch closed to passengers in 1930. It reopened to passengers from 1941–47, terminating at Friary, and closed completely in 1962. *Tony Harden collection*

Right: Hooe Bridge had a central swing section (L) that was operated by hand by the Turnchapel signalman on the swing section itself. The scene looks late Victorian. The quarry that became Bailys wood yard is still producing stone with a tip for loading into sailing ships. The foreground track may already have been connected to the L&SWR towards Oreston. The Beattie well tank is hauling a rake of four-wheel birdcage stock (not flat-roofed). The stove pipe chimney, dome positioning and type of safety valve may offer further clues of identity and dating. Any suggestions, please? *Derek Tait collection*

Below: Class O2 tank No 30182 calls at Oreston with a set of gate stock. The L&SWR faced major competition on this peninsular from both buses and ferries to the city centre. Note the vegetables and Scammell mechanical horse. © *Bluebell, JJS 1950*

The single line tablet is surrendered as class T1 tank No 80 terminates at Turnchapel. Everything looks spick and span in this L&SWR scene. The line continued through a cutting and tunnel behind the camera for freight to Turnchapel Wharf, which was owned latterly by the Admiralty. There were bases nearby for both seaplanes and submarines with fuel oil sidings and great storage tanks alongside Turnchapel station. When these tanks were bombed in 1940, the station buildings were destroyed in a fireball. The branch closed to passengers in 1951 and to all traffic in 1961. © Lens of Sutton

North Quay of Sutton Harbour was served by both the GWR and L&SWR. In this busy scene, possibly early twentieth century, coal is being unshipped, then weighed on the quayside and carried in bins to the warehouse. Maurice Dart collection

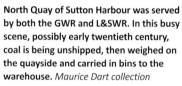

Bibliography:

Smith, Martin, An Illustrated History of Plymouth's Railways, Orwell Press, 1995.

Mills, Bernard, Steam Around Plymouth, Tempus Publishing, 2003.

Mitchell, V and Smith, K, Branch Lines Around Plymouth, Middleton Press, 1997.

Devon Galleries, Cornwall Railway Society website.

Abbreviated Credits:

Bluebell   The Bluebell Railway Museum Photographic Archive
AFP   Alan Postlethwaite
CH   Colin Hogg
JJS   John J. Smith

Class WC No 34002 *Salisbury* departs from Totnes. From about 1940, in case of line closures, certain trains between Plymouth and Exeter were headed by locomotives of the other company. This allowed crews to 'learn the road' of the other route. Possible hazards were snow, flooding, landslides, rough seas, accidents and enemy action. *© Bluebell, CH 1958*

Through Newton Abbot, Spam Can No 30 *Watersmeet* will take us back to Exeter, the Dartmoor Ring complete. *© Bluebell, CH 1958*

Ashurst Crossing
a New Forest Idyll

Jeffery Grayer

Jeffery Grayer recalls the latter days of steam at Ashurst level crossing situated on the fringes of the New Forest on the Southampton–Bournemouth mainline.

Ashurst level crossing was situated on what was then a minor road linking the A35 and the A336. Today the crossing is no more and a new road, the A326, crosses the railway by means of an overbridge to the south of the former level crossing.

Holding up a couple of cars of the period, Eastleigh-based Standard Class 4 2-6-0 No 76016 clatters over Ashurst level crossing, seen in its bucolic setting on a sunny August day in 1963, with a stopping service to Bournemouth. Today a housing estate occupies much of the area of unspoilt country seen in the background.

Cows graze and contentedly rest seemingly undisturbed by the passage of Merchant Navy class No 35019 'French Line CGT' during August 1963. Only two more years of active life remained for 35019 before withdrawal came in September 1965.

The former crossing keeper's house is seen opposite the box in this view of Standard class 4 No 76005 passing over the crossing in 1966. In connection with the Bournemouth electrification, colour light signalling was introduced between Totton and Brockenhurst 'A' box on 23 October 1966, thus eliminating boxes at Woodfidley Crossing, Lyndhurst Road and here at Ashurst crossing. At the same time automatic half-barriers were installed at Ashurst and the days of the crossing keeper vanished. Ashurst crossing was in later years closed completely and the road diverted.

Left: Original Bulleid Pacific No 34066 *Spitfire* passes the home signal, and its replacement colour light bracket, the latter awaiting its new signal fixture, with an up semi-fast to Waterloo in 1966.

Below: Bulleid West Country class No 34008 *Padstow* has charge of the premier train of the line, the 'Bournemouth Belle', having just passed the crossing, seen in the background, en route for Bournemouth in 1966. At this time No 34008 was allocated to Nine Elms depot.

The diminutive crossing box is seen to advantage in this view of Standard Class 4 No 76019 heading light engine towards Southampton in August 1963. The box contained eight levers – No 1 operating the gate lock, No 2 the gate stops, No 3 the Down distant, No 4 the Down home, Nos 5 and 6 were spare, No 7 the Up home and No 8 the Up distant.

To conclude, a fine panned shot taken near the crossing showing Merchant Navy class No 35019 *French Line CGT* passing at speed with an up service in August 1963.

The Railway and the Cross-Channel Steamers
at Littlehampton, 1862–82

John H. Farrant

The Railway Bypasses Littlehampton

(Editor's note: In 1974 Littlehampton Urban District Council produced a small booklet under the general heading 'The Littlehampton Papers No 4: Mid-Victoria Littlehampton' and with the main title below. Unavailable for some years and likely unknown of by many, it dealt with the ferries from Littlehampton, the town's attempt at establishing itself as a cross-Channel port and the subsequent involvement of the LBSCR. SW reader Mike Griffin alerted us to its existence and a quick bit of detective work allowed us to contact the original author, John Farrant, who has not only kindly consented to this reprint but also provided an updated and where necessary corrected text. Dealing with the period primarily from the middle to the end of the nineteenth century, illustrations are necessarily scant but we hope the reader's indulgence may be given with the accompanying selection of general LBSCR shipping views from the collection of the late R. C. Riley. The editor would also like to thank Arun Council and in particular Amanda Harding together with Jennifer Mason at the Sussex Record Society, all of whom assisted in locating Mr Harding.)

The Steam Packet public house in Littlehampton is virtually the last reminder in the townscape that at one time scheduled steamboat services operated to the Channel Islands and France from the erstwhile railway wharf, now beneath the approach road to the bridge opened in 1973 across the Arun.[1] While the boats ran, from 1863 to 1882, the volume of shipping using Littlehampton harbour reached a peak exceeded neither before nor since, with the possible exception of some years in World War I when the harbour was requisitioned.

The first 40 years of the nineteenth century saw Littlehampton's population nearly quadruple, as the town was established as a genteel, middle-class, seaside resort. The pace of development slowed markedly over the next 20 years. For this the railway may be held mainly responsible, as on the one hand a line from Brighton to Chichester was opened in 1846, and on the other no branch line to Littlehampton was constructed for

The first train for Bognor recorded at Barnham Junction on 1 June 1864, a scene similar no doubt to that at Ford when the branch to Littlehampton had opened in August of the previous year. The locomotive is No 29 *Escus*, built in 1843 for the London & Croydon Rly. *H. J. F. Thompson*

another 17 years. Proposals for a line to Littlehampton were first made, however, in 1845, by two companies: the Dorking, Brighton & Arundel Atmospheric Railway, to run from Dorking and branch south of Horsham down the Arun and Adur valleys, with the Littlehampton terminus near the station as eventually built; and the London & Brighton Railway, to run from the line to Chichester, parallel with Wick Street to a terminus in River Road. The latter line was authorised in 1846, but fell a victim in the collapse of the 'Railway Mania' in 1847. On the West Coast line to Chichester a station at Lyminster served Arundel (2½ miles distant) and Littlehampton (1¼ miles). The population stagnated: after a 40% increase in the decade 1831–41, it rose only 7% in 1841–51, and dropped 4% in 1851–61 (for Arundel the corresponding percentages were -6, +5, -10). The port's trade was adversely affected; in 1850, the harbour dues were reduced in an attempt to compete, and the number of cargoes entering the river from the sea fell by perhaps 20% in the course of the 1840s. Traffic on the Arun Navigation above Pallingham Quay fell by a third between 1847 and 1852, though there was a partial and temporary recovery thereafter.[2]

Nevertheless, despite a reduced income or because the debts contracted in 1826–7 had been paid off, the harbour commissioners embarked on capital works again, in 1851. These were principally to raise the west groyne (which was covered at high water) to the same height as the pier. About half the groyne was raised in 1851–6, which was probably all that the commissioners felt able to afford. But in 1859, the railway company wanted to reduce the width of the opening for shipping at Ford bridge, which, as originally proposed, had been the cause of the commissioners strenuously opposing the Bill for the West Coast line in 1844. The commissioners now agreed to the reduction provided that a railway was made from a convenient part of Littlehampton harbour through the Arun valley via Arundel to join the Mid-Sussex line near Pulborough, with proper accommodation for the reception and transit of merchandise, and with fair charges for wharfage and carriage. The LBSCR accepted the terms, should the line be continued beyond Pulborough. Powers to make the extension were obtained in 1860. Expecting increased traffic for the harbour when the railway was complete, the commissioners finished heightening the groyne in 1861–2, the total cost since 1851 being some £4000. They also dredged the mouth to deepen it by some two feet.[3]

Thus in 1863 the harbour was probably more capacious than it had ever been before. The piers were 125 feet apart, but the west pier now extended some 200 yards further seawards than the east, so as to accumulate the beach and sand working up from the west and prevent their being washed into the entrance. The east pier was continued by its groyne almost to low water mark. These works, however, did not prevent there being a shingle bar just beyond them, which was almost dry at low water on a spring tide. But at high tide there were between 11 and 16 feet of water over the bar, and several more feet between the works and in the harbour. Vessels drawing up to 14 feet could proceed to Arundel and berth piles were provided if they had to stop for the tide.[4]

The Coming of the Railway

The railway line was opened in August 1863, to a station conveniently placed in Ferry Road (now Terminus Road), between the ferry and the junction of High Street and Surrey Street. Eight months later, in April 1864, Harvey's shipyard launched a 5 to 600 ton vessel, an occasion to draw a crowd to Littlehampton. The *West Sussex Gazette* reported:

Those from the country who have not visited Littlehampton of late must have been struck with the vast improvement which is taking place round the river there. The railway wharves are completed, a steam crane is erected for unloading vessels, and there are now running to and from Littlehampton steamers for Jersey and Honfleur. The consequence of this is that a vast amount of business has been brought to the port, and houses are springing up rapidly around to meet the commercial growth of the place. In fact there is an air about the town which bespeaks that ere long Littlehampton will grow vastly in importance as a commercial port. So clearly is this fact established that the Custom House has been removed from Arundel and placed on the wharf of the railway company, so that no impediment shall accrue to the business of the port in this direction.[5]

The 1860s was indeed a decade of great change for the town. The census of 1871 duly showed an increase in population of 39% to 3,272 over 1861, and the town's renewed vitality as a resort was reflected in the construction of the Esplanade in 1867–68 and the inauguration of a local newspaper in May 1869.[6] No doubt the LBSCR's hopes of profit were pinned on traffic generated by visitors and middle class residents, but the agreement with the harbour commissioners obliged it to provide inter-change facilities between ship and train, and the more traffic the better. The Act enabled the company to purchase the river bank north of the ferry for about 150 yards, with an average depth of 80 yards back to the railway line into the station, from which sidings ran to the wharf.[7]

The LBSCR already had 20 years' experience of operating in connection with steamboats and occupied wharves in four locations, two on the Thames at Deptford (principally for landing coal from the north east for distribution over the company's network) and Battersea, the other two in Sussex. The company's first line had been from Brighton to Shoreham, linked by an incline plane to a wharf at Kingston, which was extended in 1843 to provide accommodation for the Dieppe boats of the General Steam Navigation Company. The branch line to Newhaven opened in December 1847 gave the LBSCR the opportunity to build lines right up to the river's edge, with plenty of space for expansion and also a greater depth of water. So from 1849, it connected with steamers running between Newhaven and Dieppe. In 1850, a service to the Channel Islands was introduced at Shoreham and transferred to Newhaven in 1851.[8] From that date until 1863, all the steamboats from Newhaven were operated by Henry P. Maples (with a sleeping partner named William Mories), in close conjunction with the LBSCR. But in 1863, the railway company obtained parliamentary powers to own and operate steamboats to Dieppe on its own account, and jointly with the Compagnie des Chemins de Fer de l'Ouest (the Ouest, or Western Railway of France) bought Maples out of that route with effect from 1 July.[9]

The SS *Honfleur* at the railway wharf at Newhaven sometime between 1886 and 1897. Built in Dundee in 1875, she operated regularly out of Littlehampton from 1875 until 1882 and at 229 tons was the largest steamer to do so. This was also the second LBSCR vessel to bear the name, the first based at Littlehampton in 1865–66 and sold in 1869. *(Peter S. Bailey)*

In November Maples transferred the Channel Islands service to Littlehampton because the route was shorter. 'The important addition to our district, by the establishment of a continental steam packet service', reported the *West Sussex Gazette* of 19 November, 'was inaugurated by the arrival of the first cargo-boat, the *Vibourg,* from Jersey and St. Malo, on Wednesday of last week, with a cargo of wine, brandy, eggs, fruit, etc. By great dispatch, the cargo was discharged in time for the *Vibourg* to sail on her return voyage in the evening; and on the Saturday at three o'clock in the afternoon, the first passenger and cargo boat (the *Rouen)* sailed for St. Malo and Guernsey.' The *Vibourg* was in fact advertised as carrying third class passengers, the *Rouen* and *Alar* (soon to replace the *Vibourg* and previously run by Maples to the Channel Islands from Plymouth) both second and third class. Through tickets from London to Jersey, Guernsey (though the boats do not seem to have called there regularly) and Saint-Malo were offered.[10]

There were two other operators out of Littlehampton in 1864. One was of little significance both then and for the future: the *Antagonist,* a wooden steamer of a mere 30 NRT, ran to Ventnor, Isle of Wight. The service was announced as daily, Sundays excepted, and she ran between 9 May and early September, when she was briefly succeeded by P.S. *Ursa Major,* 82 tons. Whereas they cleared with cargo or passengers on 128 occasions, they returned thus only 32 times, and not surprisingly the service was withdrawn at the end of the summer season.[11]

The other was not particularly long lived but was important for the direction of future development: this was the Littlehampton, Havre & Honfleur Steam Ship Company (LHHSSC). Probably the company's formation was under discussion before even the transfer of Maples's Channel Islands service was considered. Certainly back in January 1863, the LBSCR directors declined to guarantee 5% was registered, and soon after a second prospectus offered shares. The LBSCR objected to the statement in the prospectus that the railway company 'have laid down Rails to the waterside at Littlehampton, and are erecting buildings and forming spacious quays for the use of steamers.' 'If it is intended,' said the railway's directors, 'to refer to the steamers of their Company, such a statement is incorrect, and … this Company has no intention of giving their Company, any exclusive privilege either at Littlehampton or elsewhere.' Nevertheless, an agreement existed by February 1864, when wages began to be paid by the railway on behalf of the LHHSSC. The number of steamers which entered Littlehampton from foreign ports in 1864 was 128; Maples's operations, with a weekly service for the first five months and a twice-weekly service for the rest of the year, account for, say, 83 entries only. The LHHSSC, using chartered boats, may then have been running a weekly service from late February, perhaps with cargo only: no advertisement appears in *Bradshaw* for a passenger service.[12]

The articles and memorandum of association show the company to have been formed by a group of London businessmen with no apparent local connections; Thomas Isemonger of Littlehampton was named as a director in the articles but by October had been replaced. The authorised capital was £150,000 in £10 shares, only half of which were offered in the first issue. A return to the Registrar of Companies in January 1865 states that 7495 shares – only five short of the entire issue – had been taken up and calls of 15% had been made, £7,277 10s. having been received with £3,972 10s. outstanding. But the accompanying list of shareholders accounts for only 392 shares, of which the majority, 235, were held by Alfred Elborough, gentleman of 17 Kings Arms Yard, London; no one else held more than 25, and no shareholder lived in Sussex, though two were from Honfleur, Matthias Ullern (a director), merchant and British Vice-Consul, and E. L. Lethbridge, merchant, of whom more is recorded below.[13]

The money was to be used to build two iron steamers with first and second class accommodation, to run from Littlehampton to Honfleur via Le Havre, so bringing the latter ports within eight hours of London. The Ouest, it was stated, had linked Honfleur with Caen, Cherbourg, Brest, Orleans, Bordeaux, Nantes, Bayonne, Pau, etc., while communication with Spain and Portugal was in prospect. The case was thus based on Honfleur's rail links with the Atlantic provinces of France and the possibility of their extension further south.[14]

But why should Honfleur be chosen when the main port of the north French coast, Le Havre, lay on the opposite side of the Seine estuary and for long had had a packet service with Southampton, in connection with the railways on both coasts since 1847? The answer lay in the high cost of shipping goods through Le Havre. Rail access, particularly from the south, was poor. Within the town the lines did not run to the quays, the only route out of the town had many viaducts and tunnels so could easily be blocked by accidents, and the Seine was only crossed at Rouen. The costs entailed could be borne by the staple trade of the port, high value goods, particularly from the colonies, destined either for re-export or for Paris and the industrial areas to the north, goods which came in vessels needing Le Havre's deep water berths. But the potential traffic of the Atlantic provinces was agricultural produce which was perishable, of low value, and, so far as it passed through Honfleur and was destined for export, was carried across the estuary by small steamers and trans-shipped at Le Havre to vessels which did not need the depth of water obtained there.

Honfleur was thus the most easterly port with reasonable access to the west of France. Its harbour was 'sheltered by the land on all sides, and the wind never raises such a sea as to make it dangerous to enter.' The depths of water over the bar were similar to those at Littlehampton, but in addition there were three small wet docks, and the volume of shipping was considerably greater, 1583 vessels, excluding the steamers from Le Havre, entered in 1855, when the population was 9016. The crossing to Littlehampton was as short as any to an English port, and Littlehampton was in the right direction for the important London market. In addition, both had only just

J. P. Knight (1828–86) was appointed traffic manager of the LBSCR in 1869 and general manager the following year, a post he held until his death.

been reached by the railway, Honfleur in July 1862, so at neither was there an entrenched cross-Channel operator, though a British interest existed at Honfleur in the growing imports of coal. So the company had a fairly sound rationale for the company promoting the service.[15]

But now that railway companies were able to gain powers to own and operate steamboats, the LBSCR was determined to run its own services from Littlehampton as it did already from Newhaven. A Bill for this purpose was introduced into the House of Commons in February 1864. As the Bill was unopposed, the records of its passage through Parliament are uninformative, but several amendments were evidently made. In an attempt, no doubt, to prolong its existence, the LHHSSC successfully requested the LBSCR to insert a clause authorising it to guarantee or contribute to the capital of any company or individual undertaking any of the objects of the Bill. The Commons restricted the places to which services might run to Le Havre, Honfleur, Saint-Malo, Caen, St. Peter Port and St Helier, and deleted Cherbourg, Portrieux, Treguier, Morlaix, Brest, Carentan, Fécamp and St. Valery. The Lords reduced the maximum charge per mile for second and third class passengers from 2¼ d. and 1½ d. to 2d. and 1¼d; the first class charge was 3d. The LBSCR was empowered to raise £100,000 of additional capital by ordinary or preference shares and, after the shares were sold, £25,000 on mortgage; in both cases the money could only be used for the purposes of the Act, which was gained on 30 June 1864.[16]

The LBSCR found itself exercising its new powers sooner than probably intended. On 13 December 1864, the board directed the traffic manager 'to proceed on the principle of the Company themselves putting on steamboats to ply from Littlehampton', doubtless as the LHHSSC had given notice that it was withdrawing its service at the end of the year. As an official receiver seems to have been appointed in the following month, there can be little doubt that the company made a substantial loss on its service. In the next week, the board learnt that Maples had given notice to terminate the Jersey/Saint-Malo traffic agreement at the end of February 1865: presumably he was making no profit either.[17]

Nevertheless, the LBSCR was undeterred and inaugurated the second phase of cross-Channel steamer traffic from Littlehampton with chartered boats, probably in January 1865 to Honfleur (twice a week until January 1866, thenceforth three times), and on 1 March to the Channel Islands and Saint-Malo (twice a week). Fairly substantial capital investment was undertaken. The *Ida* was purchased for £3600, was fitted with new boilers and entered service in May 1865. In April two twin-screw steamers were ordered from the Millwall Ironworks Co. Ltd. and named *Honfleur* and *City of Rennes*; they were commissioned late in 1865. Sheds were erected at Honfleur and Saint-Malo, and additional grande vitesse vans (rolling stock for carriage of parcels) were ordered.[18]

The half-yearly report to shareholders in July 1865 anticipated a 'satisfactory return.' It failed to materialise and in November 1866 the board decided to withdraw all steamers from Littlehampton with effect from 1 January 1867. The identifiable loss which had to be written off amounted to £7165 over the two years, and related only to wages, fuel and other variable operating costs, thus taking no account of depreciation, insurance, etc., or of administrative overheads. But the loss was evidently incurred on the Jersey/Saint-Malo traffic, and a service

to Honfleur was continued from Newhaven by two of the boats transferred from Littlehampton; the third joined the Newhaven-Dieppe fleet.[19]

Regular services from Littlehampton, however, were not at an end. E. L. Lethbridge, the company's agent in Honfleur, thought he could make a profit from them and proposed, in April 1867, to charter the *Ida* for £100 per month and run her between Littlehampton and Honfleur at his own risk, with the same frequency as the company had provided. The proposal was accepted and the service from Newhaven withdrawn. The company seems to have acted as Lethbridge's agent in paying the wages of the crew.[20]

In July 1867, the shareholders voted a new board of directors to office, on account of the company's declining profitability; the board then set up a committee to inspect the company's system.[21] Early in October, it visited Littlehampton and reported that it was abandoned as a packet station by the late Directors. It was absurd to expect remunerative Passenger Traffic by this route; but it is clear that Mr. Lethbridge is making a very good profit by carrying goods from Honfleur in our little steamers the *Sussex* and *Normandy,* and that it would put us to no more expense than we incur at present if we carried this traffic ourselves, in as much as we undertake the booking and invoicing at present. Moreover, we are informed that we carry all the goods brought by these steamers along the line without charge and that we collect the debts and do the agency business for Mr. Lethbridge. These terms seem (to say the least) very extraordinary and we recommend that when the present arrangement expires at the end of the year the whole matter should be reconsidered and more advantageous terms obtained, and failing that the Company again take to the boats, and carry on the trade. Mr. Lethbridge does not insure these boats and in the case of loss the Company have nothing to look to but a nominal insurance on that myth our insurance fund.

The attempt to obtain more advantageous terms was singularly unsuccessful. A formula accepted by the board in January 1868 required Lethbridge to pay, on a (very low) valuation of the ships at £4,000, 5% for interest, 7½% for depreciation, 4½% for repairs and maintenance and 5% for insurance, a total of 22%, or £880 a year. In addition he was to pay over to the company one-fifth of through rates for all goods carried over the line and one-third of the agreed through fare for passenger traffic. The company was to maintain the boats, though the control of boats and crew rested with Lethbridge. Appointment of captain and engineer was subject to the approval of the company, which provided for the half-yearly Board of Trade survey. A fortnight later, however, the board was told that the continuance of the previous year's terms would bring in £1200, Lethbridge keeping the boats in repair. Presumably because the share in the through rates and fares was not expected to yield more than £500, an alteration in the agreement was ordered.

It seems that by the beginning of 1868, Lethbridge was handling both goods and passengers, using two boats, whereas he had started with one boat carrying goods only. During 1869 he reverted to the original arrangement of chartering the *Ida* only because he took delivery of a boat of his own, the *Caroline*.

The success of Lethbridge's business may have been more apparent than real. If it was real, he did not enjoy it for long, for he died on 1 March 1870. On the following day, J. P. Knight, the traffic manager, was endeavouring 'to make temporary arrangements for the working of the traffic pending the settlement of Mr. Lethbridge's affairs which are left in a very confused state' – so confused that the *Caroline* was seized by his creditors. A boat had to be chartered to maintain the service during the summer, and the company entered into litigation with the mortgagees of the *Caroline;* it also had to acknowledge responsibility for Lethbridge's debts with the Ouest which were finally settled at £863 in 1876.

In the following month, Mr. Frank Lethbridge, evidently the son of E. L. Lethbridge, was appointed as the company's salaried agent at Honfleur. Thus in the period of seven years the services between Littlehampton and Honfleur had passed through three different modes of operation: by a company independent of the railway (though perhaps with some agency services provided by the latter), by the railway directly using its own or chartered vessels, and by a semi-independent operator, who in the main chartered the LBSCR's vessels; and then operation reverted to the railway, and so remained until the services were withdrawn twelve years later.

By the summer of 1870, the other main element in cross-Channel services from Littlehampton had fallen into a regular pattern of operation which was continued into the 1880s. This was the Channel Islands service, which the LBSCR had abandoned at the end of 1866. From 1868, it ran during the summer, principally (at least in later years) to carry the 'early' crops of potatoes which were dug from May onwards, before crops on the mainland could be harvested. In the first year, however, William Congalton, a London shipbroker, operating under the name of the Littlehampton & Jersey Steam Packet

Company, advertised for passengers and offered through tickets via the LBSCR, and likewise in 1870, when he had been succeeded by the firm of Deacon & Isitt. In 1868, the number of entries by steam ships from the Channel Islands was 44, in 1869 it was 33, and in every subsequent year up to 1882, the number was between the two.[22]

Of the composition of the traffic carried through Littlehampton by the steamers during the first seven years, little is known, though there can be no doubt that the goods imported were predominantly agricultural and dairy produce, generally similar to the traffic which is recorded in some detail from 1873 onwards and is described in a later section. Exports were considerably less in quantity than imports, but nevertheless sufficient to make an important difference: in 1860–3 there were no exports, in 1864 they were valued at £37,556.[23] The harbour commissioners reaped a healthy increase in dues collected when the steamers were introduced. From nearly £1700 in 1845, the total receipts had fallen to around £1100 in 1856–57; thereafter, they increased (perhaps due to the carriage of materials for building the Mid-Sussex railway) to just under £1500 in 1862. The steamboat operators then used their bargaining power to secure a reduction of the dues with effect from 1 February 1864: from 3d. to 2d. per ton on the registered tonnage of all vessels trading to the port, and from 1s. to 6d. per ton on virtually all the goods which the steamers were to import, while coal, timber and building materials, hitherto the staple of the port's trade, continued to pay 1s.[24] The receipts nevertheless rose to £1954 in 1864, £2368 in 1865 and £2522 in 1866, the peak which coincided with the LBSCR's operation of both Honfleur and Channel Islands routes; thereafter, receipts declined to, in 1870, the level of 1845. The fall in 1870 was particularly because of a further reduction of the dues on vessels' registered tonnage, from 2d. to 1d., under pressure from the LBSCR.[25]

In terms of tonnage, the steamers doubled the volume of shipping entering the harbour, but as their turnaround was so much quicker than that of the sailing ships already using the harbour – at most about five steamers were employed at any one time – there were not the problems of congestion which the tonnage figures might of themselves suggest.

The LBSCR Steamer Services

Having resumed direct management of the steamers, the LBSCR set about providing better facilities for the traffic. The loading and unloading stage at Littlehampton was extended and a siding added in 1870, and a further siding in 1871; £400 was spent in repairing the *Ida*. There were brief negotiations with the harbour commissioners over a proposal by the company that the former should build a dock behind the existing railway wharf and extend the wharf southwards, at an estimated cost of £17,000. But though the commissioners had acknowledged that 'the time has now arrived when facilities may be reasonably expected to be given to the steamers frequenting the Harbour,' they were probably taken aback by the cost – and discovered that their Acts of Parliament precluded them from undertaking such works on private land. The LBSCR for its part was unwilling to expend capital on that scale.[26]

Some attempt was made to attract passenger traffic, for advertisements appeared in *Bradshaw,* but these ceased after the spring of 1872, and though a few passengers continued to be carried, the route remained, first and foremost, one for cargo. The success of efforts to increase the goods traffic justified the purchase of a new boat, the *Viking,* which was put into commission in March 1872, while some £4000 was spent in 1875 on alterations and repairs to the *Ida.* In January 1873, the Secretary of the Custom House was complaining that the increased volume of imports rendered the existing accommodation for their inspection inadequate, though not for another four years was an additional wing built onto the warehouse. For a time there were boats running to Morlaix: Mr. John Mason began a weekly service in June 1872 for goods and in September for passengers. Somehow, the LBSCR became more directly involved, Knight (by then general manager) saying in June 1873 that the service 'had in a manner been forced upon us.' The company, however, had no powers to operate steamers on this route which was abandoned in September 1873 in response to representations by the Ouest, until another private operator laid on boats in March 1876.[27]

Data on the volume of imports at Littlehampton are available from 1873,[28] and the annual average of the three years 1873–5 can be taken to represent the results of the LBSCR's efforts since 1870 to expand the traffic. By weight, the two largest components of the traffic were butter (4500 tons) and eggs (4200 tons), followed by barley (2450 tons) and oil seed (1330 tons). Raw fruit accounted for about 700 tons a year, potatoes 290 tons, seed (mainly grass and clover) 510 tons, wool and woollen yarn 140 tons and wine 180 tons. Some 800 horses were the main item of livestock; deadstock comprised principally of poultry, valued at £6800, which tended to be shipped for Christmas consumption.[29] The imports were thus overwhelmingly agricultural produce from Normandy and Brittany, and the quantities of manufactured goods were insignificant by comparison, 317 tons of glass and china being the main item. None of the imports were of particularly high value,

so the LBSCR had little scope for charging differential rates for carriage, and the bulk of the goods were seasonal, perishable and sold in competition with home produce and with imports through other ports.

On exports there is no comparable information, but in the main they seem to have been manufactured goods, as machinery, carriages and furniture are mentioned,[30] along with grain and oil. In July to December 1875, the total quantity of exports carried by the LBSCR steamers was 342 tons, and in the same period of 1876, 983 tons, so 700 tons a year in 1873–5 may be a generous estimate, as against imports of about twenty times as much.

In 1876–77, there were some changes in the composition of the import trade. The number of horses fell away to under 300 and to negligible proportions after 1877. Italian eggs began to compete with French and cut imports at Littlehampton to about 60% of their previous level, but, by passing through Dieppe, greatly increased egg imports at Newhaven. Potatoes almost ceased to be received from France, the trade perhaps being captured by Shoreham where the quantities imported showed a strong upward trend from 1876. On the other hand, poultry was on the increase, so was wine, and 1200 tons of a new cargo, sugar, appeared in 1877. This was probably sugar imported to Le Havre from French colonies, refined, and re-exported; the British import duty had been removed in 1874. But a couple of optimistic expectations were not fulfilled. In August 1875, in a (successful) attempt to get the dues reduced yet again, the LBSCR told the harbour commissioners that a large trade in barley from the Angers region which currently went via Nantes to Bristol and Southampton, and onwards to the Midlands, could be diverted to Honfleur and Littlehampton;[31] and in November 1877, Lethbridge hoped to secure 6 to 7000 tons of eggs and butter which each year were carried in sailing vessels. Though on balance the total volume and value of imports from France fell (the value from about £1.5m. in 1873-5 to about £1.2m. in 1876–7), the company seems to have been unconcerned, as the decline was attributed to the general depression of trade.

The schooner *Margaret John* (154 tons, left), and the brigantine *Gensing* (224 tons) were typical of the type of vessels operating the coasting trade to Littlehampton in the 1870s and 1880s. They were owned by Joseph Robinson of Littlehampton and Thomas Twaites of Brighton respectively, and are seen here loading ballast by River Road. The site was later occupied by Messrs Duke & Okenden and MacWester Marine Ltd. The date is after 1876.

H. J. F. Thompson

'In consideration of the satisfactory manner in which they had operated the Honfleur traffic in 1877,' the directors paid bonuses to Lethbridge and his chief clerk. But that was the last year yielding a profit. In April 1879, Knight considered the Honfleur figures for 1874 to 1878 and pronounced those for 1878 to be unsatisfactory. The principal reason for the financial deterioration was competition.

The route had never been immune from competition which was of two types, the one arising from the relative costs of sea and rail carriage, the other from more than one company operating over similar sea routes. With regard to the first, the merchant in, for example, Angers with barley for the breweries of Burton-on-Trent could choose from among a number of alternative routes and his decision was probably influenced primarily by cost, though speed and convenience played a part. He could maximise the sea carriage by sending the barley to the nearest port, Nantes or Saint-Nazaire, and shipping it to, say, Bristol, or he could minimise the sea carriage by using the railway to Honfleur and then from Littlehampton. Other alternatives lay in between: by sea from Saint-Nazaire to Southampton, for instance.

The Loire valley was the limit of the Ouest's system and hence the southern limit of the area from which the Honfleur service drew traffic. The company had only branch lines to Saint-Nazaire, Nantes, Angers and Tours, and the main line down the valley and the system to the south were operated by the Orleans Railway. Hence when, in 1876, Messrs Duche & Sons proposed to run their boats from Saint-Nazaire to Littlehampton rather than to London, the Ouest requested the LBSCR not to give encouragement because of the competition with its lines to Honfleur and Saint-Malo. Probably the Saint-Nazaire traffic directly affected the LBSCR as efforts were made to draw traffic to Honfleur from further afield: the consignments of barley from Angers anticipated in 1875 did not materialise and in January 1877 the through rate for its carriage was reduced.

Competition of the second type had always been present. Indeed, the LBSCR was the newcomer to an established pattern of services. Southampton had for long been the English port trading with the French coast westwards from Le Havre to Saint-Malo, with Weymouth sharing the Channel Island traffic. Steamers had been running from Southampton to Le Havre from 1823 and to the Channel Islands and Saint-Malo from 1824. From its earliest days the LSWR was involved with this traffic and from August 1848 had powers to operate boats on its own account.[32] In July 1863, the chairman of the LBSCR said that the company's boats were not intended to compete with the LSWR's, though the latter company evidently felt otherwise and began to operate boats for goods only to Honfleur in late 1865 or early 1866.[33] Nevertheless, from at least 1871 the two companies had an agreed tariff for goods from Honfleur. It is not surprising that in the mid-1870s, for which comparable figures are available, Southampton's imports of agricultural produce from France far exceeded those at Littlehampton with, for instance, five times as much butter and twice as many eggs; and at Honfleur alone the

LSWR seems to have had more traffic in that it normally ran four boats a week against the LBSCR's three.

The competition from these two directions limited the traffic which could be built up by the LBSCR. The competitor which appeared in August 1878 threatened to reduce even that traffic. The threat came from the boats run between Weymouth and Cherbourg by the Weymouth & Channel Islands Steam Packet Company, with a subsidy from the Great Western Railway which negotiated an agreement with the Ouest for agency and connecting rail services. In the previous March the Ouest notified the LBSCR that negotiations were in progress, and the latter was satisfied with the sole safeguard that the Ouest could not be compelled to send anything between London and Paris via Cherbourg. Indeed the LBSCR officers initially concluded that they had nothing to fear as the new route's rates were not lower than their company's. But their optimism was short-lived and within two years negotiations were in progress with the LSWR for a complete revision of the Honfleur tariff. The LSWR was worse hit, having operated between Southampton and Cherbourg since 1869. The particular reason to which they were willing to ascribe the success of the Weymouth company was preferential treatment from the Ouest, whose officials, it was said, were enlisted as canvassers for the Cherbourg route, and which sometimes carried goods to the port by passenger train.[34]

How justified these assertions were is hard to tell, as they come from the minutes, written in the LBSCR offices, of the Continental Conference. Necessarily, if the LBSCR was to exert any pressure on the Ouest, it had to argue that the Ouest was violating its obligations under the agreement for the Dieppe-Newhaven traffic which consequently was suffering loss, as the Ouest had no responsibility for the Honfleur traffic. Thus we find that on 2 April 1880 Lethbridge told Knight how the whole of the Angers district had been lost to Honfleur, that seven days later Knight told the Ouest how seriously the traffic from Brest and Angers via Dieppe was affected, and that in February 1881 the Ouest, stating it to be established that the rates between Angers and London via Cherbourg were based on those via Honfleur, argued that the Honfleur line, not the Cherbourg, was forcing a reduction in the Dieppe rates.

The fact of two English companies operating to Honfleur made it more difficult for either to compete effectively with services from other French ports, as the Ouest would make an operating agreement with neither: in 1885 the Ouest claimed that a joint traffic agreement, such as existed for the Dieppe-Newhaven route, could not be negotiated with only one of the English companies, and similar proposals were declined in 1876 and 1879. Further, not merely could the Ouest calculate that there was more profit in working only with steamer companies which had a monopoly of regular operation from a given port, but its policy seems to have been to effect agreements with a given English company in respect of only one port within the Ouest's area.[35] As the bulk of the cargo passing through all the ports concerned originated on its system, the Ouest was well able to ensure that healthy competition was maintained among the English companies; this in turn kept the cross-Channel tariffs down and increased its own competitiveness with the Orleans Railway whose system overlapped with the Ouest's in Brittany and the Loire Valley and likewise served Brest and Saint-Nazaire. Dieppe was the port at which agreement was made with the LBSCR; with the LSWR, it was Saint-Malo; with the GWR, it was Cherbourg. When the LBSCR sponsored the Littlehampton-Morlaix line in 1873, the Ouest strongly represented how it damaged its traffic to Saint-Malo, and the LBSCR withdrew from Morlaix, though exacting a promise of co-operation in a service from Cherbourg whenever the LBSCR should decide to start one. Doubtless the Ouest raised no objection when the LBSCR in 1876 reconsidered a Morlaix service, as by then negotiations had begun, on the Ouest's initiative, with the GWR over Cherbourg.[36]

Furthermore, at Honfleur there was a serious operational problem. Whatever the advantages of Honfleur over Le Havre for the export of agricultural produce, the facilities at Honfleur were still not ideal, as direct rail access to the quays was lacking there also. Goods had to be carted for a mile from the railway station, and the Ouest and other French authorities took at least five years to meet the English companies' request for lines, which would necessarily run through the streets of the town and so were not welcomed by the local residents. The hopes expressed in 1875 of bringing more barley through Littlehampton were subject to the provision of facilities at Honfleur, probably a reference to the laying of rails to the quay.

Littlehampton town and harbour in 1887, taken from the Admiralty chart surveyed by W. E. Archdeacon. The representation of the town is not accurate in all particulars; for instance River Road on the east bank south of the ferry is not marked although its buildings are. The features marked are mostly those visible from the sea.

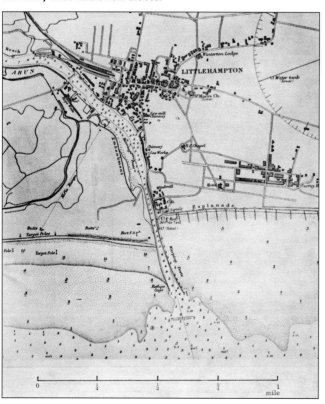

The cartage through the town was costing the LBSCR over £1000 a year in 1877, and in 1879 was being done 'in an abominable way by the present contractor.' The lines were finally opened in May 1880.

On the other side of the Channel, a service through Weymouth had intrinsic advantages over those through the Sussex ports, once the problem of the GWR's broad gauge had been eliminated in 1874. The sea crossing was shorter, and Weymouth had better access to certain English markets.[37] The LBSCR officers mentioned the loss of cargoes destined for the north and west. From Littlehampton and Newhaven, goods for the Midland and northern markets had to be transferred to another company's system in the London area, and only from 1876 was there through running (via Croydon and Willesden) from Littlehampton, and similar arrangements dated from only a few years earlier at Newhaven. Running to the west was possible only over LSWR and GWR lines. But the GWR could run from Weymouth over its own system to Bristol and make a simple link at Cheltenham with another system to run on to Birmingham. Inroads were also made on traffic destined for London, in part, though, because the LSWR from 1878 ran its fruit trains into Waterloo station which was nearer Covent Garden than the LBSCR goods station. In 1865, an Act had been obtained authorising a line of railway which could have meant that this locational disadvantage of Littlehampton with regard to the Midlands and north would have been reduced. The line proposed was an extension of the Chichester and Midhurst branch of the LBSCR to the LSWR line near Haslemere. It appears that the ultimate goal of this scheme was a connection with the GWR at Basingstoke, but it all came to nothing, probably because of the ejection of the directors of the LBSCR in 1867 and the subsequent economy campaign.[38]

The net profit in 1877 was £398. In the first eight months of 1879, there was a net loss of £3290, and, in the corresponding period of 1880, of £2620. The fall in traffic, though, was not very substantial, except in the first year of competition, 1879:

Table 1
Main Imports to Littlehampton from France, 1873–1880[39]

1873–5 tons	1876–8 (average)	1879 (average)	1880
Butter	4487	4151	3241	4015
Eggs	4197	2371	1740	1779
Barley	2456	1493	1072	1419
Oil seed	1328	1023	584	688
Raw fruit	705	880	575	637
Seed	514	401	126	145
Potatoes	289	80	156	1271
Wool & woollen yarn	142	167	157	207
Wine	180	285	183	144
Wheat flour	19	228	-	2
Sugar	-	1008	1774	1999
total tons	14317	12087	9608	12306
Horses no.	800	202	3	1
Poultry £	6800	12874	18676	29653

Some of the efforts to gain cargoes were successful, of sugar and potatoes for example, but long cherished plans to carry more fruit by running steamers direct from Duclair (50 miles up river from Honfleur) came to nothing because, it was said, the crops were so poor in 1878–80. A promising, but short-lived, development was a coastwise liner service from Littlehampton to Dublin, Belfast and Glasgow by Murray & Sons, aiming to carry French produce which previously had not reached Ireland and Scotland because of the long rail journey. But the steamers ran for only a few months after their introduction in September 1881.[40]

The financial loss must therefore be attributed mainly to the reduction in charges and a failure to reduce substantially operating expenses. It was for example only in January 1881 that a reluctant LSWR agreed to reduce the number of crossings each week from four to three.

There was one final factor which spelt the doom of the Littlehampton–Honfleur service. In 1878, the LBSCR embarked on a large-scale development of Newhaven harbour, which would give sufficient depth of water to allow sailings at all states of the tide and therefore to a fixed timetable. The large investment of capital entailed greatly enhanced the economies of concentrating all the LBSCR's steamer services there, to give maximum usage to expensive facilities, and as early as June 1877, a year before the Act to authorise the works, Knight stated the definite intention to move the Littlehampton service to Newhaven at the earliest possible date. Accordingly, on 31 August 1882, the *Rennes* and the *Ida* were transferred to Newhaven and the services between Littlehampton and Honfleur ended.[41]

The Harbour's Trade in 1880

The cross-Channel steamers formed only one element, albeit a very important element, in the traffic of Littlehampton harbour between 1863 and 1882. To set the steamer traffic in a wider perspective, all the shipping movements in one year, 1880, have been analysed in some detail.

The earliest complete year for which the harbour master's journal survives is 1880.[42] The journal appears to record the entrance and clearance of every vessel except those exempt from harbour dues (such as off-shore fishing boats), with date, ship's name, registered tonnage and, in general terms, cargo. From the 'Shipping Intelligence' of the *Sussex Daily News* has been extracted the ports from which the vessels came and to which they were bound, and occasionally more specific information about cargoes. As the column was not printed with complete regularity, being squeezed out particularly by news of the General Election early in the year, only about 90% of movements are listed. Some gaps for vessels registered at Littlehampton were filled from their statutory Log Books and Accounts of Crews and Voyages,[43] and other gaps by reasoned guesses. The analysis concentrates on the nature of the traffic entering the harbour in 1880, rather than on clearances, as imports were of greater importance than exports; when clearances are referred to, they are the clearances of those vessels which entered the harbour in 1880 (and may have cleared early in 1881), rather than the clearances in the calendar year.

LBSCR ship *Newhaven* at her home port and with the marine workshops of the LBSCR on the quayside behind.

Table 2 Entries to Littlehampton Harbour in 1880

nature of traffic	number of entries	aggregate tonnage	number of different vessels
LBSCR steamers	199	38399	4
Jersey potato steamers	36	4829	4
Baltic & deep-sea sailing ships	51	9436	49
coal imports	102	14931	54
other coastwise trade			
–from north of London or Land's End	27	2617	22
–South Coast; near French ports; Channel Islands	65	3325	28
sub-total for trade or repair	480	73537	162
yachts	13	249	10
tugs	4	34	2
windbound	10	*526	10
total in journal	507	74346	**181

* no tonnage is given for one vessel.

**this column does not add as some vessels are counted in more than one category.

If ten vessels which were windbound or stranded are excluded, vessels made 497 entries into the harbour for the purposes of trade or business (e.g., provisioning, ballasting, repairs) and are listed in the harbour master's journal for 1880. It is apparent that the harbour master did not record all entries of yachts and tugs, and if these latter are subtracted, 480 entries were made by vessels to unload and/or load cargoes, or, in two cases, for repair. The traffic can be subdivided as in Table 2.

The importance of the LBSCR steamers in the harbour's traffic is immediately apparent, as their entries represent 52% of the total tonnage. Three of the 199 entries were for vessels coming from Newhaven; the remaining 196 were from Honfleur. The number of trips in each month reflected the availability of cargoes from France. In January to March the basic service of three sailings a week was provided, but the average for June, July and August rose to five a week, to cater for the fruit and vegetable crops, and four for the rest of the year, with 19 sailings in December with seasonal cargoes of poultry and mistletoe.

Four steamers were used, though usually only two were operating from Littlehampton at any one time. They were the *Ida* (registered tonnage of 170), *Honfleur* (229), *Rennes* (219) and *Viking* (101). The *Ida* was not in service until May and her place was taken by the *Honfleur* and *Viking*. The *Rennes* was in service continuously until late August, when the *Honfleur* relieved her, and the latter and the *Ida* then operated out of Littlehampton for the rest of the year. The history of the *Ida* has been mentioned above. The other three were cargo vessels built for the LBSCR and the *Rennes*, built in 1865, was the first twin-screw steamer (the others were single-screw) to be employed on a cross-Channel route, but though she could reach a speed of 13 knots, compared with 7 to 9 knots by a single screw, she was presumably not a success, as no similarly driven vessel was introduced for 20 years.[44] Maintenance was done at Newhaven, where the LBSCR's extensive marine workshops had been opened in 1878.

All entries from Honfleur are recorded as being with general cargoes. The main items making up those cargoes have been listed in Section 3. Sometimes passengers are mentioned. If the figures for those travelling via Newhaven in 1886–9 are any guide, the number in 1880 via Littlehampton did not exceed 400 in each direction.[45] Nearly half the sailings, on the other hand, were in ballast, and probably many of the other sailings were with very little cargo, given the paucity of exports.

The Jersey potato traffic was conducted by four steamers, though only three at any one time: the *Ilen* was wrecked on a return voyage and replaced by the *Sumas*;[46] the other two were the *Drumtochy* and the *Seine*. Their registered tonnages were between 126 and 141. The first cargo arrived on 27 May, the last on 15 July. On their 36 voyages, they brought 2771½ tons of potatoes.

The Honfleur and Jersey traffic through Littlehampton lasted for only twenty years. Its departure restored the pre-eminence of the coal trade – the staple for nearly every south-coast port which was not a cross-Channel terminus. The quantity received coastwise in the Customs Port of Littlehampton, which extended from West Worthing to Bosham, was probably at its peak around 1860; then the inroads of the railway into this traffic began to outpace the increase in consumption. From 56,403 tons in 1867, shipments dropped to 35,403 tons in 1880, though thereafter levelling out; the proportion of the 1880 total which entered Littlehampton harbour was probably about 24,000 tons, sufficient still to ensure that after the removal of the steamer services, the coal trade was the main component of the traffic at Littlehampton.[47] Nearly two-thirds of the 102 shipments came from Sunderland, and those from other ports on the Durham coalfield brought the total from the north east to about three quarters; the other quarter were shipments from south Wales ports, principally of culm which probably went to the gasworks and lime burners. The only colliers regularly working to Littlehampton were those locally owned and loading at Sunderland – the *Uncle Tom* and *A. H. Locke* of Mrs. Mary Ann Lawson, coal merchant of Littlehampton (eight trips each), and the *Arun* (five trips) and *Lois* (three trips, also trading to the Baltic) belonging to Charles Henley and William Fry, respectively, merchants of Arundel. Otherwise only a couple of vessels brought more than two cargoes to Littlehampton. Having discharged their coal, the great majority returned in ballast to the port whence they came, or a neighbouring port. No more than ten managed to pick up return cargoes of timber or scrap iron. An even smaller number cleared for specific ports where they probably took on a cargo for the coal port, such as granite from Guernsey, but perhaps twenty, particularly those from south Wales, cleared 'seeking' for cargoes.

The rest of the coastwise trade can be divided between that from ports between London and Land's End and the opposite side of the Channel, and that from further north. The division is a natural one, as in 1880 no entries were from ports between Plymouth and Newport, Mon., on the west, and between London and Middlesbrough on the east. From the western seaboard came slates from Portmadoc and Bangor (ten cargoes) in vessels of about 70 tons, iron goods from Port Talbot and Newport (three) and salt from Runcorn (two), from the east, iron goods from Glasgow and Middlesbrough (two) and soda from Newcastle and Shields (three). The Welsh boats invariably cleared 'seeking', and the soda carriers discharged only part of their cargoes and proceeded westwards; a couple took on timber for the north-east. No locally registered vessels were employed, and repeat voyages were few.

The south-coast trade, on the other hand, was principally in local boats, sailing barges of 35 to 65 tons, constantly entering Littlehampton. The extreme example was John Warner's *Emma Maria* of 35 tons, which entered Littlehampton seventeen times with ashes and timber from Southampton (six times), stone from Weymouth, Swanage and Portland (eight times, on four of which to Arundel) and similar cargoes. The *Maggie* of 46 tons, built and owned by John Harvey, went further afield, bringing stone from Weymouth, but also cement from London. For both vessels, the only outward cargo carried with any regularity was chalk to Southampton. John Harvey's *Annie*, 64 tons, brought stone and wood from Plymouth, stone from Penryn, Weymouth and Guernsey, and timber and oats from London. His barges *Susie*, at 68 tons the largest regular trader, and *Sallie*, 64 tons, brought similar cargoes to the *Annie*'s. These five vessels, four of them owned by John Harvey, accounted for forty of the south-coast entries. Otherwise vessels of similar tonnage brought one or occasionally two cargoes, including five consignments of drain pipes from Poole and between five and ten cargoes of corn from

London. Clearances were usually in ballast, to the area of the port of departure. The figures in the table include two large vessels (164 and 283 tons) towed in for repair from Le Tréport and Newhaven; otherwise the only entry from France was a 33-tonner with a cargo of barley, and the Channel Islands sent two cargoes of stone from Guernsey.

A rough comparison can be made between the volume of coastwise traffic in 1880 and 30 years before. The railway may have caused a drop of about 20% in the number of cargoes received coastwise at Littlehampton during the 1840s. The Navigation & Shipping Returns for 1850 record 199 entries of vessels in cargo, with an aggregate tonnage of 21,471, but some types of cargo were excluded. Comparable figures for 1880, some 157 entries of 18,098 tons, suggest a continued decline, but at a slower rate, with vessels on average increasing in size.

The Baltic trade was if anything on the increase, perhaps encouraged by the railway. The entries in Table 3 by Baltic vessels are analysed in that table, which shows that the cargoes were exclusively of corn and timber, the staple exports of the Baltic. Corn arrived throughout the year, but the timber trade was seasonal, with most of the cargoes arriving between May and November. Timber occupied the majority of the vessels, and also the larger ones. As to clearances, over half, some 27, of vessels entering from the Baltic cleared in ballast for Elsinore (Helsingor) in Denmark, at the entrance to the Baltic, where they probably picked up orders from their owners as to the next voyage; eleven returned to Norwegian and Swedish ports, one to Abo, and one towards the Atlantic, for St Thomas, British West Indies. The remainder cleared to English ports, mainly in the north-east, either for return cargoes of coal or because they were British colliers temporarily diverted to the Baltic trade.

The ships from Denmark were the smallest (87, 89 and 93 tons), followed by those from Norway (136, 140 and 152 tons); from St Petersburg and Riga, the vessels were between 99 and 184 tons, but over 200 tons from the ports now in Finland and from Germany. Oats from Sweden came in vessels of between 104 and 183 tons, deals in vessels of between 164 and 289 tons. Ownership was in the main evenly spread: eleven entries were made by ships of British, Danish and German registration,

Table 3 The Baltic and Deep-Sea Sailing Ships Entering Littlehampton in 1880[48]

Country of departure	Number of entries	Aggregate tonnage	Cargoes carried to Littlehampton
Denmark	3	279	286 tons barley, 122 tons oats
Norway	3	4287	69 loads sawn fir, 5 loads other timber
Sweden	30	5598	1168 tons oats, 1 load hewn fir, 7008 loads sawn fir, 262 loads other timber
Russia			
–from ports now in Finland	4	999	1312 tons oats, 1916 loads sawn fir, 227 loads other timber.
–from ports now in [Russia]	7	1097	
Germany			
–from ports now in Poland	1	219	608 loads hewn fir, 353 loads sawn fir, 20 loads oak, 22 loads other timber.
–from ports now in [Russia]	2	479	
Holland	1	337	locally owned vessel in ballast
Total	51	9436	2888 tons corn, 11,191 loads timber

ten of Norwegian registration, and six and one of Swedish and Russian. The Lois brought one cargo of deals, otherwise the only Littlehampton-registered vessel was Joseph Robinson's *Vizcaya* (287 tons) which, in making three entries from the Baltic, was the only vessel to make more than one.

On the assumption that the entries of sailing ships from foreign countries in the Navigation & Shipping Returns for earlier years were always predominantly from the Baltic, this trade had increased from, usually, 10 to 20 cargoes a year in the 1840s and early 1850s, rose to between 30 and 40 a year thereafter, dipped in 1872–5 and picked up to a peak of 50 to 60 cargoes in 1877, 1879 and 1880; thereafter the number of cargoes dropped back to the level of the 1860s. So 1880 saw a high level of imports. The timber (and the slate from north Wales) no doubt passed through the hands of the three Littlehampton firms of John Eede Butt & Sons, Duke & Co., and Alfred Evershed & Co., and was presumably redistributed via the railway. The Butts' firm was probably the largest and also had a wharf and yard on the east arm of Shoreham harbour with ready access to Brighton; it was well to the front in matters of business efficiency, for late in 1879 the two offices were connected by telephone line – three years before the Brighton exchange, the first to be permanently established on the South Coast, was opened.[49]

Quite a large number of vessels were registered at Littlehampton for a port of such slight significance: at the end of 1880 it comprised 44 vessels of 7142 tons. But the proportion of the trade which was in locally registered vessels was small, probably less than 10% by tonnage, and only about a quarter of the vessels on the register visited the harbour in that year. The explanation is twofold. Firstly, the Customs Port of Littlehampton included Chichester and Bosham, and on the register were a dozen ketches and schooners which were owned by E. J. Beale of Itchenor, by Thomas Smart, by William Smith (both of Bosham) and others, and which traded to Chichester harbour. Secondly, Joseph Robinson owned a fleet of deep sea sailing ships which had little occasion to visit Littlehampton.[50] Of the eleven vessels of over 300 tons on the register (accounting for 4473 tons of the total), he owned nine. Their activities are illustrated by the following examples. The barque *Sussex*, 334 tons, cleared Greenock in September 1880, for a round-the-world voyage via Cape Town, Rangoon, New York and Stettin, reaching Honfleur in December 1881. The *Trossach*, 552 tons, left London in October 1879 for the West Indies and returned to Greenock in June 1880. The *Lioness*, 511 tons, sailed from London to the Falkland Islands and back in January to July 1880. The *Lion*, 462 tons, was away from England for a year on a voyage to India. Only the *Vizcaya*, the smallest of Robinson's vessels, traded to Littlehampton, from the Baltic. One other, the *Tarsus*, entered in ballast after a voyage from London to Lisbon and Vlaardingen (in Holland), and the *William Miles*, owned by Robinson but registered at London, brought a cargo of coal from Goole and, at 572 tons, was the largest vessel to have entered Littlehampton harbour; these two vessels may well have come to Littlehampton for repairs under their owner's eye, rather than as part of a regular trade.[51] Other than the fact of local

ownership, the main significance of these deep sea traders for Littlehampton was the number of local men who crewed them. The crews of the *Lion*, *Lioness*, *Sussex*, *Tarsus* and *Trossach* for the voyages mentioned above amounted to 56 men, of whom 19 were Sussex born, and if a place of birth is specified in the log it is near Littlehampton. Out of 15 apprentices, 12 were Littlehampton-born.

Aftermath

The harbour commissioners made no attempts to avert the transfer of the LBSCR steamers to Newhaven. At no time in the previous 20 years had their attitude to the steamers been particularly positive. Dues had been lowered whenever the company requested, and some other concessions had been made, such as dredging of berths free of charge. But the harbour facilities were not improved to increase its attractiveness to steamer traffic. Indeed capital expenditure between 1863 and 1882 was negligible. The debt incurred in the early 1860s was paid off in 1871 and the proposal for a dock was rejected in 1872. In 1874, a consultant engineer, Charles H. Gough, reported that the east pier was in very bad condition and was kept up only by the chalk between the piles, and that the cost of reinstatement in the present form would be £3650. But he recommended that the opportunity should be taken of widening the mouth to a minimum of 150 feet, 'first, because it will be far easier and better to drive new piles entirely clear of the old ones, and to complete the new Pier before destroying the old one; and in the next place it is desirable, owing to the increased and still increasing size of vessels of all kinds, and for improving the character of the Harbour, and, thereby, of course, increasing your revenue'; the cost was estimated at £19,300. The commissioners rejected both proposals: 'it is not at all desirable looking at the present state of trade in the Harbour to entertain the alteration suggested by Mr Gough's report, it appearing to the Commissioners from an actual survey made this day that no danger is apprehended either to the Pier or works on either side of the Harbour.'[52]

The annual income from dues remained at about £1,700 throughout the decade, more than in the pre-steamer days, but with higher maintenance costs to meet. After running expenses had been met there was a surplus of only £100 to £200 a year,

Modern communication for the LBSCR cross-channel service at Dieppe and Newhaven. Seen is the wireless telegraphy mast in France and the interior of the telegraph station at Newhaven.

which would not have gone far in financing works costing £17 or 19,000. The commissioners' policy could have been different only if they had taken a speculative decision to raise loans for improvements and to hope that traffic would expand and finance them. It is improbable that such a decision would have paid off, and indeed inconceivable that the commissioners would have taken it, least of all on account of the railway steamers which were probably regarded as ancillary to the usual trade of the harbour: the cross-Channel trade was transit and did not pass through the hands of local merchants who made up the commission.

The transfer of the steamers meant a drop of about £800 a year in the harbour dues collected. From July 1883, the dues and also the rates for pilotage were increased, so that the average charge on a vessel using the harbour rose by a third to a half. One result was probably to bring a sharp drop, perhaps 15%, in the coastwise trade, though it then remained fairly steady up to 1914. A special reduction for the Channel Island potato steamers was made in 1884, but from 1885 they ran to Newhaven. With falling standards of maintenance, the commission started on the path to bankruptcy and, in 1927, reconstitution under West Sussex County Council.[53]

Another group in Littlehampton was more vocal than the harbour commissioners at the departure of the steamers. In May 1882, when the proposed cessation of Honfleur services was already known, but more on account, it appears, of the LBSCR having caused the Glasgow service to terminate, a town meeting was held and a committee appointed to take steps 'for the further development of the port and for increased railway accommodation'. In particular it was proposed to approach the Midland Railway which had secured land in Worthing and was understood to be desirous of running to a port on the south coast. No more is known, but the incident does reflect current changes in the town. As a holiday resort it had entered a new phase in the mid-1870s in which the emphasis was on increasing the amenities, with the way led by new drainage and water supply systems. In 1880, the Duke of Norfolk laid the foundation stone of the water tower. Afterwards J. P. Knight wrote to the Duke: 'As the water and drainage are, I suppose, accomplished facts, we hope to see early signs of building operations at Littlehampton, so that my Directors may follow up these essential leading requirements by the improved railway communication with Littlehampton.' The allusion was of course to the carriage of visitors to the town rather than of goods to the harbour; the former was one concern of the 1882 committee, and the interest of the Midland Railway must have been in through services to the south coast for holiday-makers.[54] The riverside merchants were becoming a less prominent group in local politics as new groups emerged to concern themselves with sanitation, fast train services to London, public entertainments, etc. The harbour commissioners encountered the changing times when the Local Board wanted to lay a sewer under the river (the commissioners objected to interference with the river for 'drainage purposes'); when Knight, in 1879, requested that in the interests of safety the east pier should be completely decked over (to which they replied that the pier had been erected for the purpose of shipping and not as a public promenade); and when, three years later, permission for a band to occasionally play on the pier was sought (and granted). The improved railway communication came in the form of a loop line, opened on 1 January 1887, which allowed direct running to Littlehampton from the Brighton and Mid-Sussex lines, whereas previously trains had to enter Ford Station and reverse out on the branch line.[55]

Though local interest in the LBSCR was increasingly focussed on its passenger services, as late as 1886 its behaviour over the steamers still aroused passions. A letter to the *Littlehampton News* referred to 'the halcyon days' before 1882 when it 'pleased the Brighton Railway Company, for reasons connected with their own establishments at Newhaven and Shoreham, and other places, to divert the traffic from Littlehampton, and by differential charges, a better train service, hotels, and other facilities to transfer the business from Littlehampton. With the boat service transferred to Newhaven the traffic on the Arun practically stopped, and by preferential charges in favour of Newhaven trade has been in every way discouraged and almost destroyed by the Brighton Company, who should have protected and developed it.' The writer proposed that a committee should collect evidence and make a complaint of undue preference to the Railway Commissioners.[56]

There need be little doubt that the allegations of preferential rates were well founded: such rates were part of the normal practice of railway companies. The aspect of the LBSCR's pricing policy which does call for comment is that the company should have run the Honfleur service for so long, continuing it from Newhaven until the beginning of the twentieth century rather than terminating it while it was still based at Littlehampton. In 1883, the aggregate loss for the 12 years from 1871 to 1882 was stated to be £20,965 – which suggests that losses were more common that profits even in 1871–6. The figure can probably be accepted with confidence even if the means of its compilation are not known, as the company's accounting system had been overhauled in 1867 with particular regard to the treatment of capital. It seems that on the operating account there was a gross profit of some £6000 over the period, but the charges for insurance (probably about 5%) and depreciation (probably 7½%) resulted in a net loss. The capital cost of the *Ida*, *Rennes* and *Viking* was given as £22,256 in 1874; the capital employed in 1883 was stated to be £31,555, perhaps those three vessels plus the *Honfleur*, as four vessels were needed to keep three in service the whole time. There was also the capital cost of the wharf and warehouse at Littlehampton (said, in 1863, to be £20,000) and of sheds and equipment at Honfleur.[57] The total capital involved may have been on the order of £50,000, so, assuming an annual dividend of 4%, the rest of the company's system was subsidising the Honfleur service by nearly £4000 a year. Operating costs were probably lower at Newhaven, but additional shed and platform space had to be provided and the traffic was no greater, as goods carried in 1888–90 averaged 12,155 tons a year. The service's continuance must therefore have been justified by the revenue earned on the rail carriage of goods brought to England by the steamers, and possibly by some strategic advantage in having a foothold in France further west than Dieppe. There seems to be a clear case of a steamer service run as a 'loss leader' to attract traffic to the railway.[58]

In 1915–16, the LBSCR ran a cargo vessel from Littlehampton to Dieppe, a service, though, which must be accounted for by the circumstances of war and was withdrawn when the harbour was commandeered. In 1914 there was a rumour that a shipping company had acquired land on the Climping bank for docks, and no doubt this was not the only occasion when hopes of commercial development of the harbour were roused. But with the departure of the railway steamers, Littlehampton ceased to be a port of any but purely local significance.[59]

The transfer of the steamers to Newhaven meant a drop or about £800 a year in the harbour dues collected. From July 1883 the dues and also the pilotage rates were increased, so that the average charge on a vessel using the harbour rose by between a third and a half. One result was probably a sharp drop, of about 15%, in the vessels bringing goods coastwise, with continuing decline thereafter. The steamers in the coastal trade from 1894 were paddle boats on pleasure trips from Brighton's West Pier. Edward Watkins and William Percy Justyn, both 'outsiders', submitted proposals in 1888 and 1890 for improvements to the harbour, but these were ephemeral schemes. Standards of maintenance fell, and by 1927 the commission was no longer able to ensure that the harbour could fulfil its drainage function, and after nearly 200 years was replaced by the Littlehampton Harbour Board, most of whose members were nominated by West Sussex County Council and district councils which were authorised to make financial contributions.[60]

Notes

This article is a corrected version of John H. Farrant, *Mid-Victorian Littlehampton: the Railway and the Cross-Channel Steamers*, The Littlehampton Papers No. 4 (Littlehampton Urban District Council, 1972; published July 1973).

Abbreviations used in the Notes. *BPP: British Parliamentary Papers. Bradshaw*: *Bradshaw's General Railway and Steam Navigation Guide* (Manchester). *JHC*: *Journals of the House of Commons*. *LN*: *The Littlehampton News, Local Guide, Directory and Visitors' Arrival List*. NSR, 'Navigation and shipping returns', *BPP*, annual. TNA: The National Archives. *WSG*: *West Sussex Gazette*. WSRO: West Sussex Record Office.

1   The Steam Packet is listed intermittently in *Kelly's Directory of Sussex* but seems to have traded under that name from between 1874 and 1878, a date compatible with the building's style.

2   The Act is 9 Vic. *c.* lxviii; a Bill for extension of time was ordered on 3 Feb. 1848 but never presented (*JHC*, **103** (1848), 143). WSRO, LH/1/1/4, 18 July 1850. NSR. WSRO, QDP/ W93, 97. P. A. L. Vine, *London's lost route to the sea*, 2nd edn (Newton Abbot: David & Charles, 1966), 243–4.

3   WSRO, LH/1/1/4, 1851–62, passim. The Act is 23 & 24 Vic. *c.* clxxi, which was preceded by a plan of 1858 which would have continued the line down River Road and Pier Road to the original gasworks (now between 47 and 48 Pier Road): WSRO, QDP /W 120.

4   Based on J. W. King, *The Channel Pilot*, 2nd edn, 2 vols (1863), 1: 205–7.

5   *WSG*, 14 Apr. 1864.

6   *WSG*, 28 Nov. 1867. *LN*.

7   WSRO, QDP/W 127.

8   H. C. P. Smail, 'The genesis of the Sussex coast lines', *Railway Magazine* **101** (1955), 671. TNA, RAIL 414/6, 9 Mar., 6 Apr., 11 May 1843. TNA, RAIL 414/282, agreement with Maples for Shoreham-Jersey service, 20 Jul. 1850. NSR.

9   TNA, RAIL 414/264, French Joint Traffic Agreement, 1 Sep. 1864, reciting previous arrangements. Shoreham Harbour Bill, 'House of Commons. Minutes of evidence taken before the Select Committee on Private Bills on the New Shoreham Harbour Bill' (privately printed, 1873), 135.

10   *Bradshaw*, Oct., Nov., Dec. 1863.

11   F. T. O'Brien, *Early Solent steamers, a history of local steam navigation* (Newton Abbot: David & Charles, 1973), 157–8. *WSG*, 15 Sep. 1864; I owe this reference to Mr. G. Young. NSR.

12   TNA, RAIL 414/803, ledger, f. 1039. NSR. *WSG*, 29 Oct. 1863.

13   TNA, BT 31/786 (dissolved company no. 463C). *WSG*, 29 Oct. 1863.

14   *WSG*, 29 Oct. 1863.

15   A. Vigarié, *Les Grands Ports de Commerce de la Seine au Rhin, Leur Évolution Devant l'Industrialisation des Arrière-Pays* (Paris: 1964), 180, 319–21. C. Grasemann and G. W. P. McLachlan, *English Channel packet boats* (1939), 119. King, *Channel pilot*, 1st edn, 2 vols. (1859), 2: 70–2; 5th edn (1888), 429–31.

16   The Act is 27 & 28 Vic. *c.* cliv. For the amendments, compare *BPP*, (Lords), 1864 (3.267), xxi 'Further report of the Board of Trade.' *JHC*, **119** (1864–5).

17   TNA, BT 31/786, gives no information on the company's failure except the Chancery decree for its dissolution on 10 Dec. 1880: the winding up thus took nearly 16 years. The latest reference I have found to Maples as a shipping agent is his organising a four-week cruise around the British Isles in 1877: *Brighton Gazette*, 16 Jun. 1877.

18   *Bradshaw*, Dec. 1865.

19   TNA, RAIL 414/803, f. 1082. Reports for half-years ending 30 Jun. 1865, 31 Dec. 1866 and 30 Jun. 1867 (printed: copies in Royal Pavilion and Museums, S385LON).

20   TNA, RAIL 414/803, f. 1566.

21   C. F. D. Marshall, *History of the Southern Railway*, ed. R. W. Kidner (1963), 1: 222.

22   WSRO, LH/1/1/5, 26 May 1868. *Bradshaw*, July and Aug. 1868, July and Aug. 1870. NSR.

23   'Commerce of the United Kingdom,' *BPP*, annual.

24   Information on the harbour dues is extracted from WSRO, LH/1/1/3-5. WSRO, LH/1/1/4, 29 Oct. 1863.

25   WSRO, LH/1/1/5, 21 Apr., 22 Dec. 1870.

26   WSRO, LH/1/1/6, 21 Dec. 1871, 28 Mar. 1872.

27   *Bradshaw*, Mar. 1872. *LN*, 25 Mar. 1876.

28   TNA, CUST 23/1-10, registers of imports by quantity and declared value, for each port, 1873-82. Import figures hereafter are from this source unless otherwise stated. In order to give quantities in tons, the following have been taken to equal one ton: 50 bushels of raw fruit, 36,000 eggs, 224 gallons of wine.

29   *Bradshaw*, Dec. 1870.

30   WSRO, LH/1/1/6, 12 Aug. 1875.

31   WSRO, LH/1/1/6, 12 Aug. 1875.

32   A. T. Patterson, *A History of Southampton 1700–1914. 1, An oligarchy in decline 1700-1835*, Southampton Record Series **11**

(1966), 127. R. A. Williams, *The London & South Western Railway*, 2 vols. (Newton Abbot: David & Charles, 1968–73), 202.

[33] *Sussex Advertiser*, 4 Aug. 1863. Marshall, *Southern Railway*, 1: 180.

[34] J. H. Lucking, *The Great Western at Weymouth* (Newton Abbot: David & Charles, 1971), 57, 62. P. J. Perry, 'The development of cross-Channel trade at Weymouth 1794-1914: geographical and operational factors', *Transport History* **2** (1969), 246–9.

[35] The archives of the OUEST have not been examined, so here its policy is inferred.

[36] Lucking, *Great Western*, 59–60.

[37] Perry, ' Weymouth'. Lucking, *Great Western*, 58.

[38] H. C. P. Smail, 'Early railway travel in Sussex', *Sussex County Magazine* **28** (1954), 364.

[39] TNA, CUST 23/1–8.

[40] *LN,* 3 Sep. 1881. NSR.

[41] D. F. Gibbs, 'The rise of the port of Newhaven 1850-1914', *Transport History* **3** (1970), 261.

[42] WSRO, LH/14/1/1, Harbour master's journal 1879–92.

[43] WSRO, SR.

[44] Grasemann and McLachlan, *Packet Boats*, 75, 77. Marshall, *Southern Railway*, 1: 275, states that steamers ran from Littlehampton to Dieppe in 1880; I have found no evidence to support this.

[45] G. W. Buckwell, 'History of the Newhaven and Dieppe service', *Institute of Marine Engineers Transactions* (1891–2), 37-8.

[46] *WSG*, 24 Jun. 1880.

[47] 'An account of the quantities of coals, cinders, culm, patent fuels … received coastwise in the U.K.', *BPP*, annually from 1871 to 1896. WSRO, LH/1/1/7, 14 Feb. 1884.

[48] This breakdown tallies with NSR, except that the tonnage in the latter from Sweden is 343 more and from Russia 343 less. Import figures from TNA, CUST 23/8; a load is a measure of volume which, in regard to fir, may be taken as equal to one ton.

[49] *WSG*, 8 Jan. 1880. C. Volk, *Magnus Volk of Brighton* (Chichester: Phillimore, 1971), 40, 45–6.

[50] On the firm, see A. W. Robinson, 'A family firm of Sussex shipowners. The story of the Robinsons of Littlehampton', *Sussex County Magazine* **12** (1938), 30–2, 91–5.

[51] *BPP*, 1883 (313), lxii.

[52] WSRO, LH/1/1/6, 20 Jul. 1876, 25 May 1874. WSRO, MP 152: Gough's report.

[53] WSRO, LH/1/1/7, 11 Jun. 1883, 10 Apr. 1884. NSR. H. C. Brookfield, 'Three Sussex ports 1850–1950', *Journal of Transport History* **2** (1955–6), 40–2.

[54] *Sussex Express*, 27 May 1882. WSRO, LH/1/17, 13 Jun. 1882. *WSG*, 26 Aug. 1880.

[55] WSRO, LH/1/16, 7, 16 Nov. 1876, 16 Oct. 1879, 17 Aug. 1882. Marshall, *Southern Railway*, 1: 235. In 1863, construction of the loop line was expected soon: *WSG*, 22 Oct. 1863.

[56] *WSG*, 13 Oct. 1886. I owe this reference to Mr H. J. F. Thompson.

[57] TNA, RAIL 414/264. *WSG*, 22 Oct. 1863.

[58] F. D. Banister, *The Modern History and Future Prospects of Newhaven Harbour, Sussex* (1884), 32. Buckwell, 'Newhaven and Dieppe service', 28.

[59] *WSG*, 3 June 1915. C. L. D. Duckworth and G. E. Langmuir, *Railway and other steamers*, 2nd edn (Prescot: 1968), 154. *WSG*, 5 Feb. 1914.

[60] WSRO, LH/1/1/7, 11 Jun. 1883, 10 Apr. 1884. 17 & 18 Geo. V, c. lxvii.

The Lost Archives of Stephen Townroe
Part 6

Above: We continue our photographic journey still at Deepdene in the Second World War and a view of the telephone exchange. Who knows what messages may well have been passed along these wires. Of particular interest though has to be the second photographer intent on recording the scene from floor level. Being 'attacked' from all angles, the poor girls would no doubt have been glad to get back to normal. (We have no inkling as to who this other photographer was.)

Right: We will return to Deepdene one last time a little later but for now it is a view from the train of the demonstration run of No 21C3 soon after leaving Waterloo on 9 November 1941. Although clearly a misty day – in the London area at least – things are progressing well for the moment. It would be all downhill later though, with No 21C3 declared a failure at Basingstoke and the train taken forward to Salisbury by an unknown steam engine before No 21C2 could be substituted at Salisbury. Presumably it was invited guests, and certainly some railway staff, who made up the passenger complement, the formation seen to include at least two Pullman cars.

To be continued in Southern Way No 42, including more accidents, 'VE' celebrations and some Eastleigh Works views.

Opposite top: **Associated with the previous view, we have a cab view of either 21C3 or 21C2 on the same day.**

Bottom: **Taken sometime between July 1941 and March 1943 – a time when enemy bombing was still a major concern – SCT has here recorded how a Southern man might deal with an incendiary bomb. The location and other circumstances are not reported.**

Right: **Away from the Southern (temporarily), as we know SCT was widely travelled during the Second World War, including when he was on an LNER test train of twenty coaches from Kings Cross to Grantham and hauled by No 2509. Here he has recorded a fitter taking the temperature of the oil of the left-hand big-end upon arrival at Grantham.**

Below: **The South Western main line at Raynes Park. SCT was evidently experimenting with a telephoto lens and has captured an approaching West of England train. The recently provided brick blast-protection surround to the signal box shows up well.**

Left: **The SCT index has this view recorded as 'portrait of E W Pearce as "driver with oil can"', a phrase that could be taken more than one way. Was Mr Pearce therefore a genuine driver, or was this person, E. W. Pearce, standing dressed to pose as a driver? (Any knowledge of said gentleman would be appreciated.)**

Below and opposite page: **Four views now of the footplate of, we assume, the same engine. These were on the same negative strip as Mr Pearce and are not referred to separately in the index. From the round 'Belpaire' firebox shape, a Schools perhaps?**

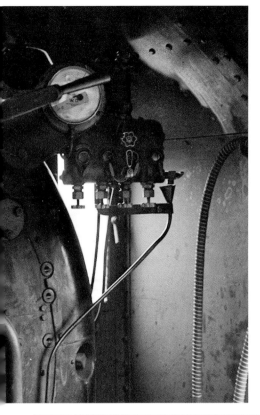

Left: As spoken of earlier, a final view of Deepdene and with it a puzzle. This is entitled, 'Wireless hut at Deepdene – showing clock'. (In another view there is indeed a view of a clock on the wall.) But 'wireless hut' and the man working at his morse tapper? Could this be the means by which the Southern communicated with its maritime fleet during wartime?

Below left: As with the view of E. W. Pearce, here we have an individual identified only as 'Pugsley' dressed as a porter and shouting 'right away'.

Below: SCT was by profession an engineer and as such was tasked with the investigation of failures. This included boiler tube failures, one example pictured here caused by corrosion and after being sectioned, photographed to show areas where the metal was particularly thin.

Below, opposite and overleaf spread: **In August 1942 an electric train derailed at Dorking North.** SCT comments that the leading motor coach came to rest 45ft from the nearest rail and on a public footpath south of the station. Recovery was by steam crane supervised by John Pelham-Maitland, who is also illustrated. ('JPM' was at the time running foreman at Nine Elms and was awarded the MBE for his work in assisting the disposal of troops from Dunkirk.) No reference to an investigation by the Board of Trade into this accident has been found – might this be as there were no passenger injuries? Of note, of course, is how the public appear to have immediate access to the DMBT coach, No 8127 from 1925 4SUB unit No 1285. In addition the window glass has been painted to increase black-out protection.

August 1942 was not a good month as shortly after the incident at Dorking came this occurrence at Epsom. As before, we have no information as to the cause/circumstances and nothing has been found so far in official documentation.

Sometime between August 1942 and March 1943 the Southern Railway was involved in the making of a 'safety first' film. Whether this was specifically aimed at SR employees or was part of a general British Railway film from the period has not been established, likewise the part played by the engine seen here. We include it as an engine in pristine condition during this period of the war was unusual, especially as SCT records it as 'being clean and in light green'. He also reports the driver as being A. Neal. There are no fewer than eighteen images of the engine and we have selected what in our opinion are the best and most interesting. One particular point of interest is the shade over the front of the cab window, an ARP precaution rarely commented upon. No location is given.

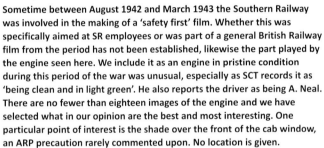

Rebuilt
The Letters and Comments Pages

As ever a bumper bundle of comments again for this issue – I'm not sure if that means there are more of you out there to comment or we have got it wrong … Seriously though one change this month, an obvious one perhaps but it comes at the suggestion of Nick Holliday. 'I have to admit I find the layout of the Rebuilt section very difficult to follow, and almost impossible to cross-reference at a later date, as so many topics are covered in a single entry, and in many cases the subject is only identified by a page number, and as each issue is numbered from 1, this doesn't help identifying the relevant article, and even worse when it is referring to a previous Rebuilt!'

A good point and so commencing with this issue we have decided to add a title to each subject together with where possible the relevant issue, and follow this with all we have received on the subject from correspondents. The contributor will then be identified at the end of his (her) quote. Obviously any feedback on this change would be welcome as well. Eric Youldon has posted a similar comment so, gentlemen, I trust the revised layout will meet with your approval.

May we also mention Rebuilt is the perfect location for that odd and perhaps unusual single image. So if you have a photograph (or two) that is a bit different in some way, we would love to see it. High-resolution JPEG scans are preferred, but old-fashioned slides, prints or negatives are perfectly acceptable. These will, of course, be returned.

We start this issue with a letter from Eric Youldon concerning a number of issues that should likely have been mentioned earlier. **(SW33/SW35)** (Eric specifically refers to comments sent that, regrettably, we can find no record of receiving, so these are therefore included verbatim.) *SW*33 refers to the two photos of E850 that actually depict E861. Questions are answered about whether No 935 had two versions of streamlining. In *SW*35, p51 claims 366 SR locos had smoke deflectors when there were actually 505. Bulleid Pacifics, 140 strong, were probably overlooked.

The eventual outcome of the trials with the LMR 2-6-4T locos was the allocation of many of the Standard 2-6-4Ts on to the Southern Region, so much so that they became ubiquitous from east to west. Here No 80016 is seen at Redhill with a train for Tonbridge. *C. R. L. Coles*

Eric also comments on **Graham Biggles' query on p39 of** *SW***39**. The 'W' tank he mentions, 31916, acquired the BR number on its bunker in June 1948 but 'Southern' on the tank survived until March 1956 when the first BR emblem appeared. The last Southern engine to retain its Southern livery in its entirety was 'P' tank No 1558, which was not changed by nationalisation until July 1953 when numbered 31558 and given the first BR emblem.

Testing the Tank Engines (*SW*39)
I would like to comment on 'Testing the Tank Engines' (Southern Way 39, pp69–70). Nos 42198/99 were both built in March 1948 (42199 in March, not April) and were indeed at first allocated to Stirling. They were transferred to the Southern Region on 14 April and returned to Stirling during the week ending 3 July. I suspect that they did not come straight from the builder to the SR – the May 1948 *Railway Observer* (RCTS) stated that 42198 (at least) had been to Stirling before moving south of the Thames. Railway enthusiasts on the Southern Region must have been intrigued to see these strangers, and indeed members of the RCTS were not slow to submit observations to the *Railway Observer*. The May, June and July 1948 issues reported on their arrival via Cricklewood on 14 April and their subsequent trials, working initially from Waterloo to Basingstoke, shedded at Nine Elms, and from Victoria to Tunbridge Wells, allocated to Stewarts Lane. As far as the 'W', No (3)1918 was concerned, the June 1948 *Railway Observer* noted that it worked a six-coach train from Ashford to Tonbridge and back on 11 May, and a special train from Victoria to Tunbridge Wells West on 13 May. *(Ross Woollard)*

The piece from the May edition (p80) of *RO* is as follows: '2-6-4T tests. On 14th April. London Midland Region Chess 4P 2-6-4Ts Nos 42198/9 were transferred via Cricklewood and the NSWJR to the SR where they are being tried in the first instance on the Waterloo–Basingstoke and Victoria–Tunbridge Wells routes respectively from Nine Elms and Battersea sheds. No 42198 was noted running in the down direction, bunker first on 19th and 20th April, passing Farnborough at about 10.34 am., and again in the up direction at 1 54 pm. The special train in each case was six corridor coachers including a Hallade recording coach. No 42199 was working empty stock trains into Victoria on 17th April and worked the 9.8 am Victoria-Tunbridge Wells West via Oxted on 19th April: trials were carried out with a six coach train including the Hallade Recorder coach, over the same route on 21st and 22nd April. The test runs were non stop, 54 minutes being allowed her the down journey and 37 for the up, the departure from Victoria was 10 3 am and return from Tunbridge Wells at 12.33 pm. No 42199 ran chimney first on the down train and bunker first in the up direction and it is understand that 42199 will undergo further trials on the Eastern section on the 8.25 am. Charing Cross-Hastings as far as Tonbridge. It may be noted that 42198 had already been to Stirling (31B) to which shed it was allocated when new in March, but with 42199 had been returned to Derby in week ending 10/4/48 for alterations to footsteps and renumbering prior to going to the Southern Region.'

(Renumbering … from what to what? And what also was the SR Hallade Recording coach? – Ed.)

Further references to the tests appeared in subsequent editions of the RO, **Neil Knowlden** having kindly supplied the relative entries from the June, July and August issues:

June 1948 – '2-6-4T Tests. Since the noted published on page 80 of the May RO, 2-6-4T's Nos 42198/9 have been noted as follows: 42198 worked the 10.54 am ex Waterloo from 26th to 30th April as far as Basingstoke, returning from there at 2.22 pm. During the five days ended 7th May, it worked Special Duty No 2 from Stewarts Lane, which includes the 8.25 am Charing Cross – Hastings train as far as Tonbridge, the 10.12 am Tonbridge – Margate as far as Ashford, the 12.40 pm Ashford – Tonbridge, and finally the 1.50 pm Tonbridge to Charing Cross. On 13th may No 42198 was observed at Gillingham (Kent) at 9.30 am on six empty non-corridor coaches running bunker first towards Chatham carrying Duty No 435, whilst on 15th May it was noted at Folkestone Junction at the head of a local passenger train from Maidstone to Dover.

'No 42199 has been used mainly between Victoria and Tunbridge Wells, having worked both the 8.50 am from Victoria via East Grinstead and then the 9.08 am via Edenbridge, the former on 20th and 21st April and the latter from 26th April. The return working of the 9.08 am is 1.08p, from Tunbridge Wells to Victoria via East Grinstead, then light engine and empty coaches to Crystal palace and Streatham Hill to London Bridge. Although officially part of Special Duty 109, the two passenger runs are referred to as TWW Duty 658, the duty number carried by the engine.

'On 22nd April, 42199 worked a special from Victoria to Chatham, and on the two following days ran between Victoria and Ashford. Both engines are now working between London and Tunbridge Wells.

'On 13th May, a special train from Victoria arrived at Tunbridge Wells West behind an SR 'W' 2-6-4T No 1918. It is rumoured that an Eastern Region 'L1' is to run trials on the Tunbridge Wells line.'

July 1948 – '2-6-4T Tests. From 4th to 16th June, LMR 2-6-4T 42198 worked on Tunbridge Wells West Duty 663 which had been specially revised to work the 7.53 am Tunbridge Wells – Brighton, then the Brighton top-link 10.50 am to Victoria via East Grinstead returning as the 3.52 pm via Uckfield, finally reaching Tunbridge Wells on the 7.34 pm ex Brighton. 42199 has been working the train arriving at Victoria at 6.18 pm from the Oxted line during the same period (duty 655).

'It is stated on p106 that 42199 was used on the 8.50 am Victoria – Tunbridge Wells via East Grinstead on April 20th and 21st. Some further details of this would be of great interest, as there is no such train as this in the timetables; whilst it is understood that certain non-passenger test runs were made these are believed to have been confined to the Hever line.

'It is understood that both LMR engines have now left Tunbridge Wells, 42198 on 19th June and 42199 the following day. The LNER L1's were expected to arrive week ending 26th June.

'On 11th May Class W 2-6-4T 31918 worked a six coach train from Ashford to Tonbridge, covering the 26½ miles in 27 minutes on the outward journey and in 28 minutes on the return run. Unfortunately further runs were not made as the engine ran hot.

July 1948 – '2-6-4T Tests. The Hallade recording car used in the preliminary stages of these tests was in use on the Western Section with 42198 on 19th and 20th April, so that it is unlikely that a special run was made on 20th April via East Grinstead. On 20th and 21st April as stated in the RO, 42199 made Hallade test runs on the direct Tunbridge Wells line, whilst 42198 was engaged on empty carriage duties at Waterloo on these days.'

Schools Class (*SW*39)

The arrival of *Southern Way* No 39 produced its usual wonderful mix of subjects, especially that of the 'School' class. Jeremy Clarke has raised the issue of why No 30925 *Cheltenham*, an example from well beyond the Southern area, was chosen for preservation rather than a member of the class named on home territory. I recall reading some time ago that the person dealing with the choice of locomotives for official preservation was aware the RCTS had been established in Cheltenham in 1928. At some point after No 925 entered service and indeed for many years after, a drawing of the engine appeared on the front of their magazine as their 'adopted' locomotive. It was this link that ensured the survival of 30925. The same official chose 30777 for preservation on the grounds of its high-speed run on the South Western main line.

On 13 May 1962 *Cheltenham* was used for a RCTS railtour, the 'East Midlander' No 5, running as 1X50 with 2P 40646 for company. This took the unusual pairing from Nottingham Victoria to Darlington to visit the Works. The return, including the racing stretch of the East Coast mainline to York, was accomplished in a shade over thirty-nine minutes reaching a maximum of 83mph. *Modern Railways* reported that after working the railtour No 30925 operated passenger services between Nottingham and Marylebone from 16 to 22 May, being based at Neasden from 17 May. It also worked a diagram covering the 6.10pm Marylebone to Woodford, then light engine to Banbury returning with the Banbury to Marylebone milk train. (At this point I commented to Frank Spence it would be wonderful to find an

Can we have too much of a good thing – I hope not. No 30939 on a Charing Cross to Dover train recorded near Hither Green and taken from an EMU travelling alongside. *C. R. L. Coles*

illustration showing the engine working on the GC, Frank then came back to me very quickly with a few other contemporary notes, which follow – Ed) The only photograph I can recall is one of her at a typical GCR station emerging from under a road bridge. I only have *Modern Railways* to consult for that era and will go through a few copies in hope of finding it.

Locospotters Annual for 1960 suggested 'Britain's most powerful 4-4-0s may soon be out of work'. Nine pages were devoted to the class, revealing interesting snippets of their work. One example deals with the fitting of the multiple jet blastpipes. No 937 *Epsom* was one of the first three to receive the fitting and on 12 July 1939 was sent out on test with the Atlantic Coast Express from Waterloo to Salisbury. This comprised twelve coaches weighing 388 tons, say slightly in excess of 400 tons with passengers. The limit for a 4-6-0 was 30 tons less. Despite signal checks, *Epsom* was into Salisbury inside eighty-five minutes. On the return run *Epsom* achieved a net time of seventy-six minutes once the effect of a special stop at Woking was taken into account. In 1960 with a Merchant Navy Pacific, the scheduled time for the journey was nine minutes more than the net time achieved by *Epsom*.

I have found a photograph of No 30925 on shed at 14D Neasden on 20 May 1962 alongside ex LMS 2-6-4T 42281. You will find it in Vol. 5 of *What Happened to Steam* that covers the Bulleid Pacifics and Schools class. It says it was there to haul specials over the GC but we know it was actually used in normal service, the only railtour being that from Nottingham. There are photos on the RCTS site covering the tour – just look at how the coal was stacked! And don't forget the Schools also went through to Oxford on inter-regional trains, as did other Southern motive power. They usually ran on the slow lines between Reading and Didcot as they did not have the Western ATC fitting. **(Frank Spence)**

The Schools Class – and in Addition Memories of the Hastings Line in Steam Days (*SW*39)

One small nit-pick to Jeremy Clarke's most enjoyable piece about the Schools class. When the Tonbridge–Hastings line was electrified thirty-odd years ago, the track through Mountfield Tunnel was gauntleted, rather than singled – operationally, the same effect, but it saved two switches and all the associated operating gear and safety features. I can't speak of the other tunnels for certain, and I assume that no changes have been made since the 1980s (I haven't had cause to travel down the line since 1989).

What follows is pure nostalgia, brought on by Jeremy's article. I always had a proprietorial attitude towards the Schools class, ever since I saw my first, No 921, *Shrewsbury, in* Second World War Southern black, bursting out of a cutting just north of Robertsbridge on a June Sunday in 1947.

I had been born and brought up on the old Met and GC Joint and had never seen a Southern locomotive (except the Met K class that might be described as honorary Southern engines, being a tank engine version of Maunsell's N class, made up of bits from Woolwich) that is until I went away to boarding school in 1944. Even then, I didn't see much Southern steam – my

school was near Sunningdale and we travelled by EMU from Waterloo at the beginning and end of term – the only thing I can boast about is that I must be one of the few of our readers who can remember 'copping' a Drummond/Maunsell Paddlebox T14, somewhere near Clapham Junction.

But our move to a small farm near Robertsbridge within sight of the Hastings main line (and the KESR) brought all sorts of delights. I came to know all the Bricklayers Arms and St Leonards Schools (occasionally spotting a Ramsgate one in London); and in the late 1940s there was even on one occasion an F1 and slightly more frequently an occasional B1 (easily recognised by the tender handrail). The slows were mostly handled by Ds (until about 1952), Ls and L1s (I never saw a D1 or E1). The freights were N1s (all six of them) or Q1s: I could spot them all from my bedroom window (a full half-mile from the line), using my great-grandfather's naval telescope, which was 3ft long.

Enough of my ramblings, but I've derived an enormous amount of satisfaction from *Southern Way* – thank you. *(Alastair Wilson)*

And along similar lines:

The image referred to by Christopher Fifield in the next paragraph. No 30938 *St Olave's* seen in Platform 3 at East Croydon on 16 April 1957 in charge of a Dover to Cannon Street (via Redhill) working.

I thoroughly enjoyed Jeremy Clarke's piece on the Schools class. It brought back memories of that 'Parly' train he mentions on p93 starting at the second paragraph. This train, usually a Schools but on occasion an Arthur, lingered in platform 3 of East Croydon for some half an hour or so from about 6.20pm, loading and unloading parcels as I (on my Mobil scooter) got to the station in time to 'cab' it (I can smell the oil and steam as I write) and then meet my father returning home from work in London off an ubiquitous 4-Sub. Later I managed to travel on the train from Tonbridge to East Croydon; it was the only train one could get from the Central Section direct to Cannon Street. I have a picture (the first I ever took I think) of it in that platform in 1957 when I was twelve. The loco was 30938 *St Olave's*, one with the Lemaitre exhaust/chimney fitted. An hour earlier the 5.25 from London Bridge (a Schools or an N Mogul – sometimes double-headed for pathing) roared through Platform 5 non-stop to Coulsdon South (!) then Redhill, where it split to Reading South or Tonbridge – this was also a 'Parly' train and its north-bound service passed through East Croydon at a leisurely post-rush hour time of about 9.45am. Another duty the 'Schools' had in the late '50s/early '60s was hauling the relief Newhaven Boat trains. **(Christopher Fifield)**

Stockbridge to Towcester (*SW*39)

The piece 'From Stockbridge to Towcester' was quite fascinating. I can't offer any specific details on either of the stations or their designer/architect. But through nothing to do with railways other than having a property of about the same age myself, I have been very surprised to learn just how organised the Victorian building suppliers and trades were during the period concerned. So I will just offer that; building material suppliers were able to supply, if you like, complete packages of materials to suit a particular design – almost like a 'kit of parts' – whereby all the specialist items such as the cast iron work and shaped bricks needed for the design would be supplied and I'll wager that this sort of service extended to all of the necessary timber work, mouldings, canopy valances and beams and windows and doors, etc, as well.

As far as I am aware these two stations are fairly unusual as far as the design of the platform canopy is concerned, in as much they are almost a combination of styles that were used elsewhere and I am left wondering if perhaps one of the buildings was perhaps a cancelled order? All the materials were on hand, then not used (perhaps with the building contractor) and thus were readily available when/wherever a suitable other location/buyer could be found? *An interesting point indeed, proving that prefabs were in fact nothing new. We are, of course, aware of similarity of buildings aka certain lines/companies whilst others appear to have been unique. I think what is unusual here is the similarity in railways many miles apart. I will use your comments verbatim.* **(Chris Sayers-Leavy)**

The Lost Archives of Stephen Townroe (*SW*39)

What a contrast the cleanliness of the U 1790 presents to the later years when I remember seeing the mogul classes. I know that labour was relatively 'low cost' at the time, but the finish can only be described as being exemplary. How times changed after the Second World War for engines of this type. Re the star 'motif' on the centre of the smoke box door, whilst perusing other SR pictures of a similar age I noticed that there was a selection of other smoke box door adornments to occasionally be seen, viz other shapes and stars of a similar size but with a different number of points, etc. Were perhaps these items unofficial adornments applied by regular crews? I suspect yes, arguably encouraged by the shed foreman to confirm 'pride in the job'.

I was quite intrigued with the smoke box picture of the T9 and its caption. I thought initially that the 'failure' referred to might be a smoke box door sealing problem, but a quick trawl of other publications that I own revealed that this combination of having two sealing systems, i.e the central dart & crossbar + lower smoke box door clamps, was quite common on a number of L&SWR loco types. The effectiveness of the traditional centre dart and crossbar method of sealing up the smoke box depends on both the door and the front rim of the smoke box being in good alignment and not being distorted. Distortion could come about either through perhaps accident damage or more likely because the smoke box ash had been allowed to build up on the inside, where it continued burning. The heat resulted in a scorched patch at the bottom of the door and then a loss of the effective seal would often occur, adversely affecting the blast pipes 'draw' on the fire in the grate and if anything making the burning ash in the smoke box even hotter. Sometimes a replacement smoke box door was fitted to regain the effective seal, but if the distortion was on the rim of the smoke box this would be more difficult to tackle and bottom clamps as shown in the picture could be used to force the door to seal tightly onto the smoke box rim. Why, I wonder, was it necessary to deploy both 'belt and braces' on these L&SWR locos?

Some designers such as Maunsell appear to have preferred the individual rim clamps for smoke box doors, although I doubt that the crews really liked them and the additional time and effort required to be able to open them! Bulleid (as ever) went one stage further than earlier designers and successfully managed to use the traditional 'dart and cross bar' arrangement on an elliptical smoke box door to good effect on his 4-6-2 designs.

Now the lifting hoist shown at the bottom of p32. This would already have been ancient when the picture was taken. But the Victorians were not known for 'cheap and nasty' at all and they built things to last, as indeed they did. Constructed mainly from timber with cast iron brackets and all mounted on double-flanged travel wheels for 'positioning', it must have kept the staff warm in the winter months operating the hoist, although some of these gantry hoists latterly had electric motors fitted to them.

Now the derailed small Prairie tank. Quite simply, this loco has 'split the points and gone down the middle'. I can't really see enough to be able to say that much more on the matter. There does not appear to be any obvious point rodding, so my assumption has to be that it was a set of hand points (which seems a bit odd in a platform area?). The point blade has not been hard against the stock rail, and the leading flange has opened up the gap as the engine moved forward. There are any number of reasons that this might have happened, but generally they all come down to poor maintenance or corner cutting by the staff involved.

Generally, to be sure that hand points remained set properly; the shunter, or perhaps in this case the firemen, should have held the lever over rather than just 'throw' the points lever and then jump back on. Thin flanges, debris on the slide chairs, poor packing or distortion/damaged point blade tip from a previous incident, or even just a broken/weak point lever spring (assuming it is a set of hand points) could all contribute to causing this derailment. The bottom picture on p33 shows the re-railing method using 'traversing jacks', which is a screw jack on a sliding base that can be wound across whilst carrying the weight that it is supporting. Looking at the picture, they are moving the loco towards the platform. Curiously, looking at the right-hand picture the loco seems to have been involved in a 'run round' movement. This suggests a 'passenger working' and in such a case I would have expected the points to have been operated from a signal box, but I'm afraid that I am not familiar with the track/station layout at it was at Chard Junc.

Opposite: **A wonderfully atmospheric capture of a 'U' class 2-6-0 awaiting departure from Victoria, destination Eastbourne.** *C. R. L. Coles*

POST CARD

THE ADDRESS TO BE WRITTEN ON THIS SIDE

The Stationmaster,
Eastleigh,
Hants.

"Highfield",
Newton Rd,
Bitterne Park
Southampton

Sir,   6/8/12.
Yesterday, I travelled
from the Docks Station,
by the 1.40. train – 3rd class,
and left the train at
Eastleigh, and forgot to
take my long black
coat from the rack.
Shall be much obliged
if you will kindly make
enquiries for me, as it may
have been kept at Waterloo
Thanking you, etc Yours truly
M. J.G. Rose.

The last sentence above from Chris '....pride in the job ...', struck a chord with something Nigel Barnes-Evans had sent in a little time ago. 'Trust of those within the job' might be an equal phrase. We trust the loser was swiftly reunited with her property.

As ever in this series of pictures, what seems to stand out above all is that everywhere is so well ordered and tidy; contrast this with today's railway. Gone today is the pride in the job of yesteryear, or is it perhaps that we are *just a more untidy race now?* (**Chris Sayers-Leavy**)

IOW O2s (SW38)

(Some correspondence on this topic has already appeared in the SW40 section of Rebuilt, but we include this piece as adding still more. – Ed.)

I have rather belatedly picked up a copy of SW38 with the Isle of Wight photographs. It's quite a challenge to work out where some of them were taken, but I've had a go even where there is not a great deal of context. I am sure you will have received many responses already, probably far better informed than me.

The view of No 19 *Osborne* on p99 is the earliest of the set. This locomotive was the guinea pig used by A.B. MacLeod's bunker enlargements in August 1932, when it was fitted with a GWR-type bunker similar to those on the large Prairie tanks, before the more familiar version was rolled out. The O2s were named from 1928 onwards, so it dates from somewhere between the two. As far as location is concerned, I think all the elements are there for this to be at the up end of Brading station – the small goods shed is just visible beyond the locomotive bunker, partly obscured by a wagon, the timber foot crossing, and the tall lattice signal post that carried the up starter and a repeater. If this location is correct, then the goods brake van is standing on the down loop, presumably while shunting is taking place elsewhere in the area.

The same location appears to be shown in the top and bottom photographs on p100, and in both of these the lower quadrant repeater is partly visible. The top photograph shows the open-fronted shed more clearly. These are later views, the locomotives being equipped with the extended bunkers.

The centre picture on p100 is of a Ventnor train standing in platform 3 at Ryde Pier Head, the key to location being the distinctive gable end to the canopy in six metal sections held together by large rivets. Locomotives could be serviced here, ash and clinker being dropped into the sea beneath the pier for the waves and tides to deal with! Platform 4 to the right was added in July 1933, so this is probably a mid to late 1930s view.

P101 proved a bit tricky as far as the top and middle views are concerned. In all probability the top view is at Ventnor, the big clue being the cliff face behind Fishbourne. There is another less likely possibility that it might be in the chalk siding at Brading. Apart from the cliff face, there is not a lot to help here. Fishbourne didn't get to the island until 1936, so the view is probably late 1930s.

I thought that I would have no difficulty in identifying a location for the middle photograph of Ventnor but I can find nothing on the main lines that corresponds with this view. This is entirely conjecture, but I wonder if the metal loop in the foreground might be a handrail for a waterfront ladder, and the track apparently half-buried might point to somewhere such as St Helens harbour or Medina Wharf? Of the two, I favour St Helens, but only because I can't find a building at Medina Wharf to match. Ventnor was also a 1936 import, which gives us a cut-off date.

The bottom picture on this page is about the easiest to locate, the distinctive roofline of Newport works in the background being the big clue.

The island O2s had cab roof ventilators fitted at some stage later in the Southern Railway period, and the rear guard irons were modified so that they were mounted on the bogie frames and not as shown in all these views on the rear of the main frames. This can give some more dating clues, but I am not sure when these modifications took place. (The exceptions were 35 *Freshwater* and 36 *Carisbrooke*, which missed out on the roof vents because they were late imports and ran throughout their lives without this modification. For some reason, 33 *Bembridge* had a non-standard roof in three sections rather than two without a vent. This begs the question as to another late import, 34 *Newport*, but this locomotive was scrapped early and I don't recall seeing any views showing the roof). By the way, what happened to 22 at Bembridge? (*As mentioned in* SW*40, the editor eats humble pie at omitting the final view of the series. It was belatedly included in* SW*40.)* **(John Burgess)**

Brockenhurst School Trains (*SW*37)

On 25 July the *Daily Telegraph* printed a reader's letter that said in the 1930s Weymouth Grammar School did not accept the sons (no mention of daughters) of tradesmen. Consequently, a large number of boys travelled daily to Dorchester, where the local grammar school was less choosy. As peak travel times, in order to relieve congestion in corridors and on promise of good behaviour, train guards would shepherd boys into otherwise empty first-class compartments, The reader did not explain if at Dorchester pupils used the Great Western or Southern station, but perhaps this was the precursor of regular school travel as described in my Brockenhurst School train article. (On 27 July 2017 the media reported that the Transport Minister, Chris Grayling, had commented that to reduce overcrowding on trains the Train Operating Companies would convert some first-class seating to standard class. He seemed to overlook the fact that some TOCs have already done this.) **(Richard Simmons)**

Also on the subject of School Trains and from John Harvey: I found Richard Simmons' article on School Trains in *SW*37 very interesting, especially that relating to the Dorchester and Weymouth area. The reason the 'Scholars' needed to travel between the two towns was because Weymouth's Grammar School was co-educational and Dorchester had completely separate grammar schools for boys and girls. Residents of Weymouth who were eligible were given a choice of the style of grammar school education. If the choice was Dorchester then travelling was required.

Those of us living in Weymouth in the years either side of 1960 who had an interest in the railway could move sharply out of school at 4pm and be at our vantage point just outside the town station in time to see the 'up' Channel Islands Boat Train (around 4.15pm), until the autumn of 1959 destined for Paddington with the change to Waterloo delayed, as I recall, by a dispute in the printing industry that resulted in certain timetables not becoming available. When the WR Boat Train did not run there was still a 4.15pm to Paddington (or at least Westbury) and the attraction of that train (can I say this in *Southern Way*?) was the likelihood of an ex-Works (from Swindon) County, Hall or Grange normally never seen in Dorset. For a period there was also a 4.30pm WR train that seemed to be mostly vans but offered passenger accommodation to Bristol. The next departure was the 4.45pm Bournemouth Central and Eastleigh train.

An interesting individual image submission from Jeff Grayer. Jeff asks a simple question, 'Does anyone know where, when or what?' Suggestions welcome.

In the down direction, the 2.55pm Bournemouth Central arrived at 4.17pm, then the 12.30pm Paddington ran in at about 4.25pm and the CWN 14 September 1959 ufn states that this train consisted of a Corridor PMV, four or five WR coaches (depending on the date) and a WR 'B' set. The CWN alleges that the 'B' set had been attached at Dorchester West, having performed as the 8.40am Weymouth–Maiden Newton, then the 9.27am Maiden Newton–Weymouth, and then the 10.40am Weymouth–Dorchester West. I have to say that I don't remember the 'B' set, but presumably the CWN's intention was for these two carriages to be available for 'scholars'. (I do remember, however, pushing the Hall, usually either 4945 'Milligan Hall' or 7917 'North Aston Hall' depending on the season, around on the manual Weymouth turntable, the Westbury crew seemingly happy for someone else to do the work).

My recollection is that the 12.30pm Paddington always looked presentable with clean engine and clean, but sombre-looking maroon coaches. Incidentally, Lancing always seemed to produce a better, brighter finish on the SR's BR Malachite coaches than the WR maroon coaches and the (theoretically?) Malachite-painted WR DMUs at that time. Anyway, as I recall, the smart 12.30pm Paddington was closely followed by a rather scruffy-looking train consisting of a Weymouth 43xx mogul and two WR coaches. I recall corridor stock, but not a 'B' set, and this was certainly locally known as the school train. As Richard Simmons says, before the 1960 summer timetable began, the 12.30pm Paddington ceased to run, but there was a 4.15pm Dorchester West that was 'Not Advertised'.

Moving on to the CWN and Engine Workings for 11 September 1961 (unfortunately the next I can access), there was a 4.15pm SX Dorchester West to Weymouth consisting, so the CWN says, of a 'B' set and two WR SK coaches. The engine was a Weymouth 43xx mogul on Duty 451, returning to Weymouth having been despatched to Dorchester South at 2.50am for carriage shunting, freight shunting and transfer freight working between the South and West yards. I don't remember four coaches on this train, or a 'B' set. Would there have been a local arrangement for this working? The coaches had earlier worked on the 8.23am Weymouth–Maiden Newton, hauled by a 41xx 2-6-2T (either No 4133 or 4166) on Duty 441 returning at 9.28am to Weymouth. I suspect that it was the 8.23am train that the scholars should have caught to Dorchester in the morning. The coaches were worked to Dorchester in the early afternoon on the back of an up train consisting of vans for Newcastle, Swindon and Bristol, plus another 'B' set.

For the summer of 1962 the Engine Workings were similar: Duty 451 and a 43xx on the School Train, but in the morning Duty 441 was changed to a 57xx 0-6-0PT and the train now left Weymouth at 8.40am, although it returned from Maiden Newton at the same time as the season before.

If one lingered on the embankment outside of Weymouth station until after 5pm, the Southern engines for the 5.35pm to Waterloo and the 5.41pm to Bournemouth Central could be seen coming off shed before pausing to back down to the station for their trains. WR DMUs ran in and out during this period, but occasional highlights in spring included van trains of flowers bound for London from the Channel Islands, and could produce an ex-Works West Country, or comparatively rare in Weymouth at the time, a Schools.

I can add a rider. Perhaps unsurprisingly, there was trouble between the boys and girls on the train and I understand that at some point in the early 1960s segregation was imposed when bus transport was provided for the girls … *(John Harvey)*

Southern EMUs (*SW*37)

It shows how second, third and even fourth 'glances' through *SW* can throw up queries. The photo on p84 of *SW*37 is one. The caption states the train is a 'Waterloo–Brentford–Richmond–Waterloo' working. So far as the headcode is concerned, that is correct and this would mean it is confined to 'The Windsor Lines'. But looking at the picture it is clear that with the sidings on the right the train is actually on the main lines through Clapham Junction. As the only other '89' coding applies to a coastal working between Portsmouth and Southampton via Netley it must be a case of mistaken reading of the duty card. As the '80' series applies almost entirely to workings around Portsmouth it seems likely the '8' is the wrong 'un, yet there is only one code ending in '9' that is applicable to local services, ergo '19', Waterloo–Epsom or Leatherhead via Worcester Park. I suspect a bit of detective work may be needed but that might defeat even Sherlock Holmes. **(Jeremy Clarke)**

Again on EMUS and but commencing with wagons: With reference to Chris Sayers-Leavy's comments in Rebuilt, *Southern Way* Issue 38, p59, regarding the logic in requiring different wheelsets for different wheelbases of LBSC wagons. I believe the

Coaling at Weymouth, 22 September 1965.

Steam and electric at Vauxhall. The now 'preserved' but sectioned No 35019 *Ellerman Line* is on the last leg of its journey to Waterloo, whilst an augmented SUB unit, including a Bulleid trailer, passes in the down direction with an 'L' headcode – Waterloo to Chessington South – service.

simple answer lies in a statement in *Southern Wagons Volume 2* (Bixley, Chorley, King, pub OPC). On p22, referring to the final batch of 500 5-plank Open A wagons ordered from the Metropolitan Carriage, Wagon and Finance Company in 1920: '... they were much more modern in design than any other LBSCR open wagons. Amongst other features they had RCH journal spacing (6ft 6in, most other LBSC R wagons employed 6ft 3in).'

This is where the wheelbase issue comes into play. These wagons, and an earlier batch of SECR design seven-plank opens from Hurst, Nelson, and probably also to RCH specifications, had a 9ft 0in wheelbase, whereas almost all other LBSC wagons were 9ft 3in, 9ft 6in or 9ft 9in. So, in general, any LBSC wagon that didn't have a 9ft 0in wheelbase would require a Brighton-specific wheel set, whereas those that did could be fitted with RCH standard ones. Nothing to do with solebar material or loadings.

Re *Southern Way* Issue 37 and the piece on Southern Multiple Unit Photography, the caption writer has got a bit confused regarding the converted LBSCR South London Line overhead stock. On p24 the units pictured are correctly identified and described as 2-SL sets, although the note that they were confined to the South London Line is demonstrably incorrect, because these units appear again on p26 and 27 on the West Croydon to Wimbledon line! However, on those pages, they have been incorrectly named as 2-Wim – the dropped roof at each end being an easy identifier.

The associated notes regarding the 2-Wim evolution are wrong. They started, like the 2-SL units, as part of the original three-coach sets for the South London Line overhead electrification, with their distinctive, and unique, square panelling style and heavy underframes. In service it was quickly noticed that the provision of an entire coach of first-class compartments was unnecessary, the service only required two coaches for most of the day, and the use of two powered units in a three-coach train was overdoing things. The first-class centre coaches were removed and new composite non-powered driving trailers were built, to a completely different design and width, to create twice as many two-car units, which could be run as four- or six-coach trains during the rush hour.

The redundant first-class coaches were eventually adapted for mainline use, which duty they carried out for nearly twenty years, but their excess width meant that they were rather restricted in use. Presumably the creation of the 2-SL units and the impending electrification of the West Croydon–Wimbledon line inspired Brighton and Lancing to take in these coaches and transform them into the 2-Wim sets, with some reconfiguration of compartments to accommodate drivers and electrical equipment. The roofs were treated to domed ends similar to those on the later 2-Bil sets, resulting in quite an attractive outfit. After running-in on the South London Line, they took up their duties from Wimbledon, which they carried out until 1954, by which time the 2-SL units had joined them on the line. Their extreme 9ft 6in width had restricted their use to the two lines, and required careful route planning whenever they travelled south for attention. **(Nick Holliday)**

Brought Back to Life
The Story of Just One Wagon

Chris Sayers-Leavy

A picture appeared on the back cover of *SW*39 that brought back some happy memories for me of a project that I was involved in many years ago now. The image showed an ex-LBSCR 10-ton, round-ended, wooden-framed goods wagon being loaded or unloaded on the Corringham Light railway (CLRly) in Essex.

What you might wonder was my connection with this picture, which was taken some thirty years before I was born? I certainly was not even aware of the tenuous CLRly connection myself, that is until this picture was published ...

Well the story for me goes back some forty-two years to 1975 (just writing these numbers down makes me feel quite old all of a sudden) when I was a volunteer on the Bluebell Railway. At the time everybody was well aware that 1975 was 150th anniversary year of railways in this country and that a cavalcade of locomotives was being organised plus a static exhibition of items of rolling stock to be held at Shildon in County Durham – appropriate as this was close to where the Stockton to Darlington railway ran. The Bluebell was still very much a 'small engine line' back then, the largest working loco being the BR Class 4 No 75027, but, of course, as one of the first standard gauge preserved lines, it also had a number of Victorian engines and one of the oldest that was in working order was Stroudley 0-6-0T A1X Terrier No 672 *Fenchurch* built in 1872.

I was based at Horsted Keynes at this time undertaking various engineering jobs and helping out the C&W Dept from time to time. Word soon reached Horsted Keynes that the loco dept. at Sheffield Park had been approached to send 'Fenchurch' up to Shildon for the cavalcade – and the C&W people, who were by then starting to turn out some excellent restorations – were not even being considered for any form of contributory exhibit for this 'big event' up in the North-east.

Understandably feeling a bit left out, there were those who lamented the fact that, whilst 'Fenchurch' would be representing the LBSCR's part in railway history' there was nothing else that we had that was deemed worthy of display to go with her. The Bluebell was, of course, still a landlocked line at this time and everything that came to the railway had to be brought in (or taken out) by road.

We had made great strides in recent years in reducing the cost of this road transport, by doing many of the smaller jobs ourselves, and one such job involved our friendly lorry driver/haulage contractor, a chap called Wally Parsons who was based at Wonersh near Bramley in Surrey, bringing to Horsted Keynes a very dilapidated wooden wagon from the closed Longmoor Military Railway.

Those of us that looked at what had arrived were very disparaging about it. At Longmoor the Army had used the wagon to dump fire box ash and clinker in and the hot ashes had burnt their way through the flooring and even through to some of the wooden framing. It was, to all intents and purposes, a lost cause. But what had caused the wagon to be brought to the Bluebell was the fact that it was actually a 'surviving' ex LBSCR wagon and whilst the Bluebell was ostensibly an LBSCR line, very little

The ex LBSCR wagon as it arrived at Horsted Keynes from the LMR. Originally built in 1917 as No 3346, it was subsequently given the SR number 22568, and then finally WD AD46269.

Stripping the wagon down, seen here placed on trestles and with the old bodywork removed.

The similar wagon at Long Marston. The comparison with the buffer heights of the vehicles either side is interesting.

company rolling stock had been acquired over the years when at the time nobody even thought people would want to see preserved goods vehicles, let alone goods trains.

Consequently there was much mumbling going on and a degree of disquiet, that is until the notion occurred to us that maybe, just maybe, the wagon could be restored quickly and sent to Shildon with 'Fenchurch'.

Well, to cut a long story short, we were told that if it could be readied in time it could indeed 'go to the ball', so to speak. Now of course, all the people with the bemoaning loud voices suddenly had to deliver on what they said they could do and a colleague of mine, Graham Burtenshaw, and I stepped forward saying that we would do the heavy work if we had the support of all the other interested parties to help us, mainly in doing the support tasks of labouring, cleaning and painting items plus organising the supply of new materials, etc. To my knowledge this was also the first real project undertaken at Horsted Keynes, where everybody from all departments lent a hand and mucked in rather than just being disparate groups with their own departmental interests.

The wagon was then first unloaded and then craned on to a set of trestles so that the frame and body could be worked on, whilst other people cleaned and painted the wheels, axle boxes, springs and brake gear plus miscellaneous iron work, etc. Once on the trestles, all the burnt material was stripped off of the frame so that a proper assessment of what was actually required could take place. This quickly revealed the result; things weren't just bad, they were *very* bad. Only one solebar was worth saving, both headstocks needed replacing and we began to wonder just what we had taken on. In addition, a complete new floor was required together with most of the body (including the bottom side rails all round). On the plus side, most of the major steel work could

be recovered/patched up, except the bolts, which were beyond recovery. Fortunately, also all the springs (six off them – four for the wheels and two for the drawhooks) were OK, as were the drawhooks themselves and buffers, but a number of the main frame (wooden) bracing struts also needed replacing. In addition it was intended to restore the rounded ends on the wagon, which not only involved new longer tapered end posts but we needed to find a new tarpaulin bar and its mountings, the originals of which had been taken off the wagon many years ago.

We did not have any original drawings for the wagon, just a picture of a similar example owned by the Army that was seen at Long Marston in 1971, remarkably with the tarpaulin bar still in place. Hence, all sizes/dimensions had to be taken off the original material that we had. Lists were then prepared and fortunately the responsibility for sourcing the materials required fell right into the lap of David Wigley of the Southern Locomotive Society, who was able to use his business contacts to be able to source the imperial sizes of material/items that were required. There were a few problems getting the right size/grade of timber needed for the main frame components and all the standard bolt sizes were either too long or too short, so I spent a lot of time cutting and welding up many of the long bolts that were required.

The Alf Brown gang took on the task of producing the new tarpaulin bar and its fittings with a bit of a lull whilst we waited for the new materials to start arriving. This lull gave us the time to dismantle the old wagon frame, which sounds simple enough. However, as you can imagine, nothing wanted to come undone and everything had to be cut in order to release bolts that had been in place for a very long time and exposed to all weathers, plus the acidic elements of wood and the ashes that had been dumped into the wagon.

With the new solebar fitted, the first headstock could be removed.

A wagon frame of this type of construction is basically all mortise and tenon-jointed and then held together with various long bolts or tie bars. It represents almost the final design of wooden wagon under-framing whereby the wagon actually 'floats' around a 'continuous metal draw bar' that connects the two drawhooks together. These are in turn linked to the horizontal leaf springs that take the shock loads from the buffers, in such a manner that the wagon's wooden frame does not take any of the haulage drawbar forces and is only in 'compression' during train braking. When it came to dismantling the frame, there was a real danger that everything would just collapse into a heap of rotten wood, so great care had to be taken to ensure that the 'assembled construction' remained square and in the shape that we wanted to maintain. This in turn meant that major frame components had to be replaced one at a time rather than just completely dismantling it all and then starting again. Once the defective sole bar and headstock had been removed (separately) it became clear that in addition to having the mortise and tenon joints on them, they were also fashioned with 'stop end chamfers' on most of their exposed edges. This is basically Victorian decoration intended to stop the edges of the 'cut' timber splitting and Graham did not have the time to be able to put it on to the new material. Fortunately a volunteer then came forward from the S&T Dept. called Roger Resch. He then undertook this time-consuming task, having previously performed the task on wooden signal posts – such was the dedication of the true LB&SC enthusiast.

Graham Burtenshaw concentrated on cutting out all of the timber joints and once he had an assembly ready I would then hastily start drilling and bolting it all together, aided and abetted by anyone else who was to hand at the time. Progress was painfully slow, to say the least, but we had to keep up the pace up if the wagon was to be ready in time to go up to Shildon.

Once the frame was completed, it was lifted off the trestles and put back on its wheels on the track, so that it could be moved under cover whilst building the body. People could then start to see that we really did stand a good chance of making it and the project seemed to get a 'second wind' when it came to building up the body, with more and more people helping out. Graham was kept busy cutting timber and I seemed to be forever drilling holes and altering the length of ⅝ & ¾in bolts. Gradually the new

The 'hot' spanner was an indispesable item for working on the wooden wagon.

Fitting the new end posts – caused a bit of head screatching.

wagon could be seen to be taking shape. A particularly fiddly job was tapering the pairs of long wooden body end posts.

All sorts of people helped out with the painting of the small parts and then the body itself. To our amazement the new tarpaulin bar arrived just when it was needed and it fitted like a dream; after all none of us had ever built a full-sized railway wagon before and we only had that 'picture' of what it should look like to go on.

As it got to the final push, activity became frantic and if you stood still for too long there was a serious chance someone would paint you. Mick Blackburn undertook to do the lettering; he was an ace restorer of enamel and station signs so he had already had plenty of practice. Then, right at the end the evening paper, the *Brighton Evening Argus*, got wind of what we were doing and sent a photographer down to see what all the fuss was about – only to find that we had actually finished all the work. Mick had to casually recreate his signwriting pose for the picture that was to appear in the paper.

So the wagon ended up being a bit like the 'Irishman's knife'; it is more than 100 years old and has only had one new blade and two new handles in all that time. Needless to say that when the wagon departed for Shildon it was a bit of an anticlimax – what were we all going to do now? And then another bright idea then came to mind and four of us who had been heavily involved in the project took a leisurely bus trip north, calling into various other preserved railways along the way, as we gradually made our way up to Shildon – in an ex London Transport 1950s central

Mick Blackburn recreating the lettering for the newspaper photographer.

area AEC RF single deck bus – culminating in a trackside view of the cavalcade parade on the last day of the festivities.

Revisiting my past activities in writing this piece has brought back a lot of memories, not the least of friends and acquaintances that after all these years are no longer with us. But, of course, the wagon lives on and it should be good for another 100 years – providing that is that they don't start dropping loco fires into it again!

The wagon is lifeted for loading onto the low loader and (right) being shunted to Shildon.

Southern Steam Operations
Supplement No 1
Ian Simpson

Since this book went to press the author has received a considerable quantity of new information. This has highlighted a few errors and omissions, as well as providing significant new material on the operation of loco diagrams and the workings of individual locos. The current errata and omissions are presented here. In addition, a very small portion of the 'new material' is selected, based on items that the author feels are of special interest.

1 Errata

Page 41 – lower photo of No 76067 at Fratton: The date was 29 March 1967 and not 9 May 1967 as shown (apologies to the photographer John Scrace for the error in transcribing his notes, which *were* correct). The photo also shows No 80151 on the extreme left. No 80151 failed on the 15.05 Andover–Basingstoke freight on 28 April and remained out of use at

Basingstoke Loco; hence the date of the photo could not have been 9 May.

The 18.09 Waterloo–Basingstoke commuter train changed from Crompton diesel plus TC sets to EMU on 12 June 1967. This is shown correctly in the main table (Table 7.1), but not in the summary table (Table 7.3b). To correct this error, the final sentence in Section 7.6 should read as follows: 'In the final four weeks of SR steam working, five commuter trains were diesel-worked (45 percent), four electric-worked (36 percent) and two steam-worked (18 percent). There is a small knock-on effect to the relative percentages of diesel and electric working shown in Tables 7.5 and 7.7 (column 12 Jun only).'

BB Pacific No 34089 *602 Squadron* in Earlsfield cutting with the 10.51 Southampton Eastern Docks–Waterloo OLE train on Thursday 6 July 1967. This train did not appear in the STAN, but Southampton Docks-related records identify that it ran for the docking of the *Caribia*. Peter King

Page 121 – caption to the upper photo of No 34009: Four (not five) WC Pacifics were withdrawn during w/e 2 October 1966. The fifth WC was withdrawn two weeks earlier. All this information is shown correctly in Table 8.1 on the opposite page.

Down relief trains on Saturday 3 June 1967: There is overwhelming evidence that No 34023 worked the 10.35 Waterloo–Bournemouth and No 34090 the 10.24 Waterloo–Weymouth, rather than the other way around as shown in Table 13.14 (p255) and in the caption to the photo of No 34090 on p260. It appears that the trains were running out-of-sequence west of Basingstoke, No 34023 (on the down fast) having overtaken No 34090 (on the down slow) in the Fleet area. Further supporting evidence is that No 34023 was turned at Bournemouth and ran light-engine to Southampton to work the 'Gresley' special from Southampton to Salisbury; hence it was more likely that No 34023 was on the Bournemouth as opposed to the Weymouth train.

In Table 14.2 (duty 412) it should read '18.30 Southampton–Bournemouth' and not '18.30 Bournemouth–Southampton'.

Caption to photo of No 80145 on p323: 'in Subsection 14.7.6' should be replaced by 'on page 258'.

2 Omissions

P38, lower photo taken inside Eastleigh Loco: The year 1967 was omitted from the caption.

Maundy Thursday, 23 March 1967: There was a ninth down relief train that was not shown in Table 11.10 (p194). This was the 16.22 Waterloo–Weymouth (Additional 1Z70), almost certainly hauled by WC Pacific No 34037.

Footnote omitted in Table 13.14 (p255): On 27 May 1967, the 09.22 down Ocean Liner Express (OLE) train was diverted from Eastern to Western Docks according to STAN p46. This is confirmed by an observer who was at Southampton Central. On the same day, the 16.30 down OLE was diverted from Western to Eastern Docks.

Ocean Liner Express (OLE) named trains (Table 7.10, p106 and Subsection 7.13.1, p105): A fourth liner (*Fairstar*) should be added to the list of those whose associated OLE trains were given the name 'Sitmar line – Australia' in the STANs. Regarding 'Royal Mail Lines', to the author's knowledge there was no 'Royal Mail Lines' headboard and the only headboard for OLE trains associated with that company was 'The South American'. After the *Andes* was converted to a cruise ship and was involved in short duration (typically two-week) cruises it is highly unlikely that 'The South American' headboard would have been carried by the associated OLE trains. Hence, although the *Andes* OLE trains were named as 'Royal Mail Lines' in the STANs, it is highly unlikely that there was any 'official' intention for a headboard to be carried.

3 New Material – Updates, Additional Information and Some Questions

The last date for a Feltham 'S15' 4-6-0 on a normal service working (Subsection 2.1.2, p32): This date now stands at 15 September 1965, when No 30839 was observed on an up freight at Sturt Lane at 07.20. Any advance on 15 September? (the remaining three 'S15s' were officially withdrawn during w/e 19 September 1965).

Guildford Standard 5 4-6-0 No 73092 in Earlsfield cutting with the 13.31 Southampton Eastern Docks–Waterloo OLE train on Thursday, 6 July 1967. This train ran for the docking of the *Flavia* which was berthed at Eastern Docks. The displayed headcode (1,4) indicates a departure from the Western Docks. A possible reason for this apparent contradiction is discussed in the text. *Peter King*

The final Guildford 'N' 2-6-0 diagrams (Subsection 2.1.3, p33): More specific detail of the working of these diagrams has become available. On SuX, 'N' duty No 181 was responsible for working the 07.30 Woking–Basingstoke stopper, returning light-engine to Guildford. On M–F from 16 May 1966, the 07.30 became a WR DMU working, but on Saturdays duty No 181 lasted until 11 June, just before the start of the summer timetable. As noted in Subsection 2.1.3, the 'N' 2-6-0s were seldom seen on the train. Of forty sightings between mid-February and 11 June, a former Southern Railway 2-6-0 was seen on only one occasion (not an 'N', but 'U' No 31639 on Saturday, 19 March). Substitute power was mainly Guildford Standard 5 4-6-0s, but Eastleigh Standard 4 2-6-0s also performed and there is one instance of the use of an unrebuilt BB Pacific – No 34066 *Spitfire*. The last known appearance of a steam loco on the 07.30 was Guildford's 5MT No 73037, on Saturday, 11 June. On Saturdays until 16 April 1966 there was another 'N' duty (No 182), which was responsible for working three van trains: 05.20 Woking–Aldershot, 11.03 Guildford–Clapham Jct and 15.38 Waterloo–Basingstoke. The 'N' class put in at least three appearances on this duty, being noted on the 15.38 vans on 12 March (unidentified 'N'), 26 March (No 31405) and 2 April (No 31411). On M–F this train tended to be worked by Guildford 5MTs, but the author can find no trace of the train in the available Guildford loco diagrams. The absence of the 'N' class from their own diagrams arose from their frequent use (together with the 'U' class) on the overnight PW ballast trains connected with engineering works for the Bournemouth electrification scheme. Nos 31408 and 31639 were still working on their 'effective' withdrawal date of Sunday, 5 June 1966, being seen at Farnborough in the morning on an up engineering train and an up breakdown train respectively.

Ocean Liner Express (OLE) trains – identification of the associated liners: In the book, the liners associated with the OLE trains were identified from SR (SWD) documentation where available, but there were a few gaps. From Southampton Docks-related records it has now been possible to identify four more liners whose OLE trains are mentioned in the book.

P106 – No 73119 with the 'Union-Castle Safmarine' headboard on Good Friday, 8 April 1966; this was the 09.20 Waterloo–Southampton Western Docks and the Safmarine liner was the *S A Vaal*.

P249 – No 34008 on the 10.00 Waterloo–Southampton Western Docks on Saturday, 13 May 1967; the liner was the *Chusan*.

Can anyone provide information as to which loco worked the 16.51 Basingstoke–Salisbury local train on Thursday, 22 June 1967?

On Sunday, 28 May 1967, WC Pacific No 34040 *Crewkerne* **underwent a transformation from the filthy external condition of previous days (when it was on the Guildford diagrams until Friday – see photo on p246 – and on the 16.20 Southampton–Bournemouth local on Saturday), to the highly polished condition depicted in the accompanying photos. All this effort was to little avail as it seems that the loco was taken out of traffic less than a week later. No 34040 is viewed inside Bournemouth Loco in 'spotless condition' in the early evening of Sunday, 28 May. The surrounding 'mobile trestles' may have facilitated the cleaning of the loco.** *Richard Weisham*

Table 14.15 (p289) and Subsection 14.8.1 (p298) identify two up OLEs on Thursday, 6 July 1967 that did not appear in STAN p56. The first OLE was hauled by No 34089 and the second by No 73092. The port docking records reveal that the liners associated with these trains were the *Caribia* and *Flavia* respectively. There was a third up train (hauled by No 34025) that did appear in STAN, p56. The docking records for the *Carmania* and train observations are all in agreement with p56 in this case. Table A summarises the details for the three up OLE trains and their associated liners. Each of the liners was berthed at the Eastern Docks. Observational evidence reveals one anomaly; Nos 34025/89 displayed the (1,6) headcode, whereas No 73092 displayed the (1,4) headcode. In the down direction headcodes (1,4) and (1,6) applied to the Western and Eastern Docks respectively. In the up direction, (1,6) was meant to apply to all OLE trains (according to the Sectional Appendix to the WTT and Ian Allan's *abc British Railways Headcodes 1965*). However, there is ample photographic evidence to show that (1,4) and (1,6) were often used to distinguish Western from Eastern Docks for the up trains too. So why was No 73092 displaying the headcode (1,4) from the Western Docks, when the *Flavia* was berthed at the Eastern Docks? The answer to this question may be quite simple. Earlier in the day, No 73092 had worked the down *Fairsky* OLE for Western Docks and bore the correct headcode (1,4) for that train (see photo in the lower half of p297). It could be the case that the crew had simply neglected to change the headcode from (1,4) to (1,6) for the return working from Eastern Docks.

Electro-diesel (ED) and Crompton Type 3 diesel diagrams in April 1967 (Subsection 12.3.1, p210 and Table 12.3 (a), p211): It has now been possible to fill in some of the finer detail in ED duty Nos 73–5 and Crompton Type 3 diesel duty Nos 39–40. As suggested in Subsection 12.3.1, there *were* workings between Bournemouth and Eastleigh; duty No 73 started with the 04.35 Eastleigh–Bournemouth freight (working in multiple with the Crompton on duty No 39) and duty No 75 terminated with a light engine movement from Bournemouth to Eastleigh (paired with the Crompton on duty No 40). Thus it seems that duty Nos 73–5 were worked as a three-day cyclic diagram starting and finishing at Eastleigh, with overnight stabling at Bournemouth on the first and second days. Duty Nos 39–40 formed a two-day cyclic diagram starting and finishing at Eastleigh, with overnight stabling at Weymouth during the intervening night. The photo of the ED and Crompton double-headed freight (see p111) is an example of a 'JB-KB' combination where multiple working with a single driver could be achieved with both the ED and Crompton working on diesel power, or, alternatively, with the ED on electric power and the Crompton on diesel power.

Nine Elms Standard 2-6-4T duties: In the book there was insufficient space to include details of the Nine Elms tank duties, except in Chapter 14 for the last four weeks of SR steam (12 June to 9 July 1967). While most of the tank duties were confined to the London area, there were two Standard 4 2-6-4T duties up until Sunday, 11 June 1967, that took these locos outside the confines of the London suburban area at weekends. Details of these duties are shown in Table B. The first 2-6-4T duty was Saturday No 102, which worked the 11.05 Waterloo–Basingstoke vans, returning light engine to Waterloo. The motive power on this van train was recorded on ten of the thirteen Saturdays between 18 March and 10 June 1967 inclusive; in each case a Standard 4 2-6-4T appeared as booked. This included No 80140 on 20 May, which almost certainly dates the photo on the bottom half of p232. The second 2-6-4T duty was Sunday No 108, which worked the 03.40 Waterloo–Petersfield passenger and newspaper van train, departing light engine from Nine Elms Loco at 02.40 coupled to the WC Pacific that was booked to work the 03.35 Waterloo–Portsmouth and Southsea passenger and van train (duty No 143 in April; thereafter No 136 from 7 May to 11 June inclusive). Perhaps the most remarkable facts associated with these duties is that the down trains both ran via Guildford over the Portsmouth direct line in closely spaced pathways and that the latter part of duty No 108 was sometimes Pacific-worked (rather than 2-6-4T-worked). Since publication of the book, Guildford-related records have been unearthed that fill in some detail about the locos that worked duty No 108. Details are shown in Table C. It may be seen that, on two occasions, the latter part of the duty was used to return to Nine Elms a Pacific that had somehow found its way onto the Guildford Standard 4 2-6-0 cyclic diagram (duty Nos 165–6) during the previous days. Correspondingly, the Standard 4 2-6-4T that was now 'spare' at Guildford Loco (having worked the first part of duty No 108) was put onto the cyclic diagram (duty Nos 165–6) the following Monday morning. Referring to Table 13.11 (p245), this explains how No 35007 was removed from the cyclic diagram on Saturday, 13 May and replaced by No 80133 on Monday, 15 May. In fact, from the augmented records now in the database, it appears that this is how No 80133 departed from Nine Elms (with the 03.40 down on Sunday, 14 May), never to return. Thereafter, No 80133 was based at Eastleigh until the end of SR steam, although the loco remained officially allocated to Nine Elms (see Subsection 2.3.5, p55).

The final workings and the withdrawal date of WC Pacific No 34040 *Crewkerne*

As noted in Section 14.1 (page 264), No 34040 was taken out of service a considerable time before its official 'effective' withdrawal date of 2 July 1967. Table D accounts for the final workings of No 34040 between Wednesday, 24 May, and Friday, 2 June. It is thought that this list is reasonably complete, but the author would be pleased to receive any additions, particularly for the period post-2 June. After working the 11.05 Waterloo–Basingstoke vans on 2 June it appears that No 34040 remained at Basingstoke Loco for a few days and was then hauled 'dead-on-wheels' to Eastleigh on 8 June (see Table E). Thereafter there are numerous sightings of it stored or dumped at Eastleigh Loco. So the question is: why did it take as long as one month from the loco being taken out of service to an official decision being made for its withdrawal? This issue might be resolved if the reasons for No 34040's demise were known. Can anyone help with this?

No 34040 departs from Brockenhurst with the 08.29 Eastleigh–Weymouth on Monday, 29 May. This train was normally the 08.29 Eastleigh–Bournemouth 'all stations' (duty No 407 for a Bournemouth Standard 4 2-6-0), but was extended to Weymouth on this Whit bank holiday Monday and booked for WC Pacific haulage in the day's special diagram notice. Presumably the train was extended to facilitate travel from the local stations between Eastleigh and Bournemouth for a day out at Weymouth on this public holiday. *Peter King*

Table A: Details for the up OLE trains on Thursday, 6 July 1967

Loco	OLE train	Pathway	B No.	Time at SL	Load	Head-code	Liner	Docking time	From	Berth No
34089 10.51 Southampton Eastern Docks–Waterloo		Q	†	13.05	2v,10c	1,6	*Caribia*	07.30	Kingston	38
73092 13.31 Southampton Eastern Docks–Waterloo		Q	†	14.57	2v,9c	1,4	*Flavia*	09.43	Sydney	32

Notes: B No. is the boat train number assigned in the STANs. Berth Nos 32–43 were in the Eastern Docks. † Not shown in STAN p56, train timings determined from the Sturt Lane (SL) passing time and the nearest Q pathway.

Table B: Nine Elms Standard 4 2-6-4T loco duties Nos 102/8 at weekends from 8 April to 11 June 1967

Saturdays		
102	Shunting Waterloo 00.00–03.00	LE
	03.00 Waterloo–	E
	Clapham Jct 03.10	M
	04.04 Clapham Jct–	LE
	Waterloo 04.17	
	06.37 Waterloo–	LE
	Clapham Jct 06.47	V
	07.20 Clapham Jct–	
	Nine Elms Loco 07.35	LE
	Nine Elms Loco 07.35–10.20	E
	10.20 Nine Elms Loco–	
	Waterloo 10.35	
	11.05 Waterloo–	
	Basingstoke West Yard 13.01	
	Basingstoke Loco	
	13.54 Basingstoke Loco–Waterloo 15.14	
	Shunting at Waterloo and various ECS workings	
	to/from Clapham Jct	

Manning arrangements for duty No 102

Nine Elms men
1. Off No 102 (Friday) work and relieved Waterloo 00.28.
2. First set on duty 23.58 (Friday), relieve at Waterloo 00.28, work and dispose.
3. Second set on duty 09.15, work and relieved at Waterloo 16.45.
4. Third set on duty 16.15, relieve at Waterloo 16.45, work and dispose.

Sundays		
108	02.40 Nine Elms Loco–	LE
	Waterloo 02.55	
	(coupled to No 143†)	PV
	03.40 Waterloo–	E
	Petersfield 05.42	
	06.05 Petersfield–	
	Guildford 06.50	LE
	Guildford shunting	E
	06.50–07.30	V
	Guildford Loco	LE
	07.35–11.10	
	11.10 Guildford Loco–	
	Guildford 11.15	
	11.38 Guildford–	
	Woking 11.50	
	12.25 Woking–	
	Clapham Jct 13.00	
	13.15 Clapham Jct–	
	Nine Elms Loco 13.30	

Manning arrangements for duty No 108

Guildford men
1. First set on duty 22.56 (Saturday), passenger to Nine Elms Loco, prepare and work 02.40 LE and relieved at Guildford 06.50.
2. Second set on duty 06.25, relieve at 06.50, work and relieved at Woking 11.50 and home passenger.
Nine Elms men
3. Off No 502 ('Warship' diesel-hydraulic duty) relieve at Woking 11.50. Work to Clapham Jct and change with No 16 (Crompton Type 3 duty).
4. Off No 16 change at Clapham Jct at 13.15 work and dispose (at Nine Elms).

Notes: † No 136 from 7 May to 11 June inclusive. Train type: E = ECS. LE= Light Engine. M = Milk. P = Passenger. V = Vans (parcels, newspapers, etc).

Table C: Locos that worked Sunday duty No 108 in April–June 1967

Sunday duty 70A/108/St4T	23 April	30 April	7 May	14 May	28 May	4 June	11 June
03.40 Waterloo–Petersfield PV	80140 (70A)†	75076 (70D)	80133 (70A)	80133 (70A)†	80015 (70A)	80085 (70A)	76026 (70F)
11.38 Guildford–Woking E	34044 (70F)‡	75076 (70D)	80133 (70A)	35007 (70A)‡	80015 (70A)	80085 (70A)	76026 (70F)

Notes: Loco numbers in bold indicate that the motive power was exactly as specified in the diagrams. Motive power for duty No 108 was not recorded on 21 May.
† The loco was removed from the diagram at Guildford on Sunday after working the ECS from Petersfield, remained at Guildford Loco, and then worked the 03.18 Woking–Fratton vans on the following Monday (duty No 165).
‡ The loco had arrived at Guildford early Sunday morning off Saturday's 18.51 Bournemouth–Woking stopper (duty No 166) and then came onto duty No 108 working the 11.38 Guildford–Woking ECS.
Locoshed codes: 70A = Nine Elms. 70C = Guildford. 70D = Eastleigh. 70F = Bournemouth.

Table D: The last workings of WC Pacific No 34040 *Crewkerne* (70F)

Day	Date	Train working or locoshed sighting	Type	Load	Shed	Duty	Class
Wednesday	24 May	10.15 Fratton–Basingstoke	V		70C	165	St4
Wednesday	24 May	14.05 Basingstoke–Surbiton	V	17v	70C	163	St5
Thursday	25 May	03.18 Woking–Fratton	V		70C	165	St4
Thursday	25 May	10.15 Fratton–Basingstoke	V		70C	165	St4
Thursday	25 May	14.05 Basingstoke–Surbiton	V	17v	70C	163	St5
Friday	26 May	03.18 Woking–Fratton	V		70C	165	St4
Friday	26 May	10.15 Fratton–Basingstoke	V		70C	165	St4
Friday	26 May	Basingstoke Loco 14.00					
Friday	26 May	16.51 Basingstoke–Salisbury	P		70C	165	St4
Friday	26 May	19.20 Salisbury–Northam	V	5v	70C	165	St4
Saturday	27 May	16.20 Southampton–Bournemouth	P	3c	70A	136	WC
Saturday	27 May	18.08 Bournemouth-Weymouth	P		70A	136	WC
Saturday	27 May	22.13 Weymouth–Bournemouth	PV		70A	136	WC
Sunday	28 May	Bournemouth Loco 18.30					
Monday	29 May	05.44 Bournemouth–Eastleigh	P		70F	407	WC
Monday	29 May	08.29 Eastleigh–Weymouth [1]	P	9c	70F	407	WC
Monday	29 May	22.13 Weymouth–Bournemouth [2]	PV		70F	407	WC
Tuesday	30 May	Early morning local Bournemouth workings?	P		70F	394	WC
Tuesday	30 May	15.01 Bournemouth–Weymouth	P		70F	394	WC
Tuesday	30 May	18.15 Weymouth–Waterloo	P	5c, 5v	70F	394	WC
Wednesday	31 May	02.45 Waterloo–Bournemouth	PV		70F	395	WC
Wednesday	31 May	07.08 Bournemouth–Weymouth	P		70F	395	WC
Wednesday	31 May	14.45 Weymouth–Westbury	SF		70A	146	MN
Thursday	1 June	07.49 Weymouth–Bournemouth	P		70A	147	MN
Thursday	1 June	12.35 Bournemouth–Waterloo [3]	P	10c	70A	147	MN
Thursday	1 June	18.54 Waterloo–Basingstoke	P	10c	70A	147	MN
Friday	2 June	07.05 Basingstoke–Waterloo	P	10c	70A	148	MN
Friday	2 June	11.05 Waterloo–Basingstoke	V	7v	70A	148	MN
Saturday	3 June	Basingstoke Loco					
Sunday	4 June	Basingstoke Loco					
Thursday	8 June	14.55 Basingstoke Loco–Eastleigh Loco, hauled dead	LE				
		Numerous sightings dumped/stored at Eastleigh					
		Loco from 14 June to 8 July 1967					
		Official withdrawal 'effective date' 2 July 1967					

Notes: The trains highlighted by grey shading are 'inferred' sightings (and therefore are not necessarily correct), the remainder are first-hand sightings.

[1] Normally an 'all-stations' train to Bournemouth booked for a Bournemouth Standard 4 2-6-0, but extended to Weymouth on Whit Monday bank holiday with a lengthened formation of nine coaches and motive power specified as a WC Pacific in the special loco diagrams.

[2] 22.13 Weymouth–Waterloo mails, double-heading with a Crompton Type 3 to Bournemouth. Normally duty 70F/404/St4, but amended to 70F/407/WC in the special loco diagrams.

[3] 11.18 Weymouth–Waterloo express.

Train type: LE= Light Engine. P = Passenger. SF = Special Freight ('Vanfits' of tomatoes). V = Vans (parcels, newspapers, mail etc).

Loads: c = coaches. v = vans. Class: St4 = BR Standard 4MT 2-6-0. St5 = BR Standard 5MT 4-6-0. WC = Light Pacific.

MN = Merchant Navy Pacific.

In filthy external condition, No 34040 is seen between Southampton Central and Millbrook with the 16.20 Southampton–Bournemouth local service on Saturday, 27 May 1967. The following day the outward appearance of the loco was transformed, as shown in the accompanying photos. *Peter King*

Table E: Extract from Special Notice No 748 SWD, dated 7 June 1967

2. Engine Hauling 34040 (Thursday, 8 June)

	9Z74	
	Arr	**Dep**
Basingstoke MPD		14.55
Basingstoke	TL	15.02
Worthing Jct	15.07	
Winchester Jct	15.40	
Eastleigh	15.55	
Eastleigh MPD	16.05	

Note: TL= Through Line

WC Pacific 34037 *Clovelly* has just passed Clapham Jct with the 11.20 Waterloo–Southampton Western Docks Fairsky OLE on Thursday, 6 July 1967. This was the second down Fairsky OLE on that day and the train appeared as the 'Sitmar Line – Australia' named train in the STAN, although sadly no headboard was carried to mark the occasion of the last steam-hauled 'Sitmar Line' OLE train. *Peter King*

4 Acknowledgements

Thanks are due to Geoff Burch, Paul Gibbons and Peter King
for providing input to this article.

Southern Way

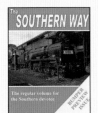
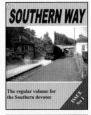

The regular volume for the Southern devotee
MOST RECENT BACK ISSUES

The Southern Way is available from all good book sellers, or in case of difficulty, direct from the publisher. (Post free UK) Each regular issue contains at least 96 pages including colour content.

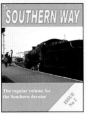

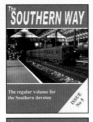

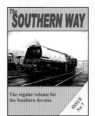
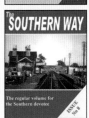

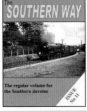

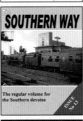

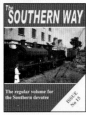

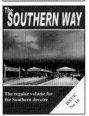

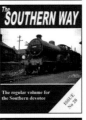
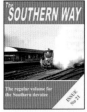

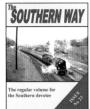

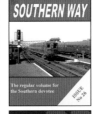
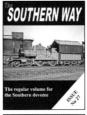
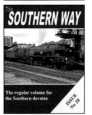
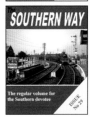

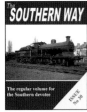
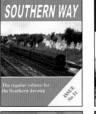

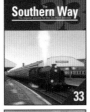
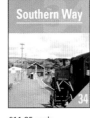
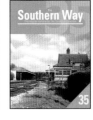
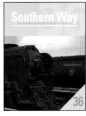

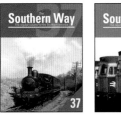
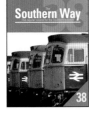
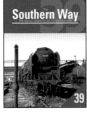
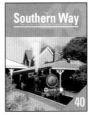

£11.95 each
£12.95 from Issue 7
£14.50 from Issue 21
£14.95 from Issue 35

Subscription for four-
issues available
(Post free in the UK)
www.crecy.co.uk

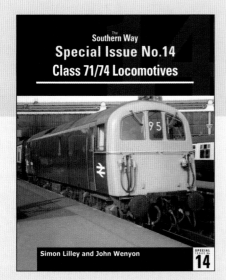

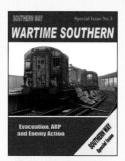
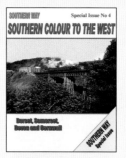

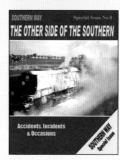
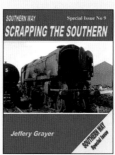

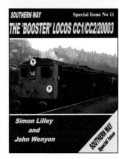